crowded tables and bonus tracks

A MEMOIR

ASHLEY McLAIN

Published by d'Aulnoy Editions
Atlanta, Georgia
www.daulnoy.com

d'Aulnoy Editions is an imprint of White Deer Publishing, LLC.
www.whitedeerpublishing.net

First edition, May 2026
Ebook edition created 2026

Cover design by Beth Gonzalez
Author photo by Sarah Bork
Edited by Lauren Kelliher, Charlotte Bleau, Telia Garner, and Emily M. Owens

Library of Congress Cataloging-in-Publication Data is on file at the Library of Congress, Washington, DC.

Hardcover ISBN 978-1-945783-56-2
Paperback ISBN 978-1-945783-48-7
Ebook ISBN 978-1-945783-49-4

For information about special discounts available for bulk purchases, please visit www.daulnoy.com/bulk-orders

This book is memoir. It reflects the author's present recollections of experiences over time. Some names and characteristics have been changed, some events have been compressed, and some dialogue has been recreated.

To J.C., Corbin, and Beckett

And to my family, my friends, my colleagues, and my tribes

Contents

Prologue

I didn't feel the urge to look for my biological parents for most of my life. I never wanted to appear ungrateful and didn't want to spread myself too thin, timewise or emotionally. I have a remarkable immediate and extended adoptive family, including my sister who is my parents' biological daughter. I've woven my adoptive mother, father, and sister throughout these chapters, which I hope convey my love, appreciation, and commitment to them.

After a chance encounter with a friend who also spent her first weeks of life at Hope Cottage (a Dallas adoption and foster care agency) in January 1968 and hearing her story about reuniting with her birth parents, I finally allowed myself, a fifty-three-year-old empty-nester, to get curious about my origin.

I started to wonder about my bio mother (my bio father was a second thought): Who and how was she? What did my biological heritage have to do with my leadership style, my professional drive, my parenting, my caution around finances, the way I stay calm in a crisis, or anything that wasn't clearly attributable to the environment in which I was raised?

Finding my biological family in 2021 — a momentous year for me at home, at work, and in the world at large — helped motivate me to start writing my story. Knowing I was adopted, I felt like a gift — a present — because my mother told me this for as long as I can remember. The value of a gift is determined by its giver and receiver. I've contemplated whether a gift in itself has any inherent value. What does it mean to me to be a gift?

Since my retirement in 2023, I have been investigating how I think and feel now, and how I felt and thought in the past. I've been compelled to get answers and tell my story. After months of writing classes and thousands of stream-of-consciousness words in my journal, I started over to tell my story from the beginning. My teachers and editors helped weave threads to bind the pieces together. This memoir includes essays in five parts: what we inherit, what we seek, what we choose, what we build, and what we understand.

These pieces are peppered with advice that has shaped my life and career. The words of people who have an impact on us resonate in our minds. Some things I've been told have become personal mantras; many are tips that I have passed along to family members and colleagues.

I recently opened a fortune cookie message that said: "To remember is to understand." In writing this memoir, I've sought a deeper understanding of myself and my life, including its fortuitous beginning, and what has occurred since, whether by fate, free will, biology, or environment. My hope is that you will find a bit of yourself here, too.

For anyone who reads this memoir — family, friends, or someone in the future kind enough to consider any light my words might shed on this time in the world — with outstretched hands and heart, I gift my story to you.

Introduction: One Life I've Lived

2023

One life I've lived is at a podium, before a crowd of several hundred people in my eye-catching salmon-orange suit. I wear the highest block heels I can walk in. I wear my don't-screw-with-me reading glasses, so I can check my notes, and so the faces of the crowd are blurry. I smile and hold my chin up, pretending I can see them. I want them to see me as a strong, proud woman who is empowered yet relatable, shining the light on the superbly qualified panelists with a bit of it bouncing over to light me up, too.

It's recalling the first day commanding a new company with my partners. I buy a $12 coffee maker, toilet paper for the bathroom, ink, and printer paper. We call and drive and meet and shake hands and smile and read and map and analyze and write and fifteen years later we've built a consulting business of 100 people among five offices.

It's in transitioning this work family we've built, this entity full of passion for the environment, people with skills and aspirations, and the company identity we created with color schemes, logos, fonts, and websites, expanding it into a reputation for excellence. It's deciding I didn't want to give my entire life to that entity. I'm the leader; I love the spotlight and sharing my passion — but I'm ready for a lifeboat.

I choose the company that speaks our work language, respects our skills, and provides a bigger stage and geography to my work offspring. I jump into that lifeboat and put on my best suit and peddle their services for a couple years. I change my language; our colors go from green and blue to orange and black. We drink the Kool-Aid, recite the core values, take the safety trainings, and I'm put in a regional leadership position. I'm honest and vulnerable and share my worries for our people during the integration. I don't love the spreadsheets enough, the gross margins and profits; I don't cut the people with institutional knowledge (who are "aging in place") for the shareholders' benefit. They judge me on their criteria and don't leverage my strengths. I'm useful to them for those couple years; then

At the podium to moderate a panel.

they offer me an orange life jacket. Step back. Step out of the spotlight, and I can stay forever.

One life I've lived is in a liminal space — I'm not what I was, but I have yet to become what I will be. I decline the life jacket. I don my don't-screw-with-me reading glasses. I take my name off the door and my vacation photos off the walls, because I have the resources to jump ship from this ungainly hulking vessel. To my people: I taught you to care for yourselves and be your own leaders. You're fully capable of charting your paths forward, wearing orange and black, or blue and green, or something else entirely.

I'm no longer at the podium, on the stage, as a leader. I put on my blue jean jacket and cowboy boots and walk away. I'm going to explore the valleys, rivers, coastlines, and mountains we've worked to protect. I take a deep breath, slow my heart rate, and gaze at the open landscape ahead.

Widening my perspective to the Steamboat horizon.

Part I: What We Inherit

The families, homes, and communities we're born into or live in during early life set the tone for our experiences. Scarcity and abundance are opposite ends of the same spectrum. I know my life has been filled with privileges.

Nurture rules with a heavy hand in our early years. I grew up with loving parents in a beautifully decorated home on a busy street in a nice neighborhood. I was a kid close to nature, eager for adventure, but socially cautious. Though several strong matriarchs nurtured me, I didn't yet know how to draw on their strengths. I lacked nothing and fit into the fabric of my family and community, so I didn't start contemplating a search for my birth mother until later in life.

Earliest days with my mom Sue; she's working on getting comfortable.

My Mother Called Me a Gift

My mother, Sharon Sue Sears McLain Dockery, is the Energizer Bunny. She's involved and engaged and interested and curious and active and stubborn and judgmental and proud. She prefers to be busy rather than lonely.

Mom dresses elegantly, carries a cute, impractical purse, always has her nails and hair done, and doesn't like ugly shoes. She consumes books. She's on the curriculum committee for the Osher Lifelong Learning Institute at UT Austin. She's the one who brings in scholars on mental health, art, science, classical music, Russia, and China, and a million other topics. She takes classes at Southwestern University in Georgetown. For years she volunteered to teach people about clean water and sanitation in Belize.

She's active in the Church on the Hill, is part of Women on the Journey, tutors a fifth-grade student at a local elementary school, walks trails, takes Pilates and dance classes. She knows the rhumba, the foxtrot, the waltz, the two-step, the tango. She goes to the ballet, the symphony, and the opera. She has sailed on Texas lakes, the Atlantic Ocean, the Pacific Ocean, off the Gulf coast, and the Caribbean. Once, in British Columbia, she helped captain and crew sail through the night avoiding floating logs from the timber harvest while speeding to a home port to avoid a major storm. She's forever talking about the next sailing trip — she wants to sail the Amalfi Coast and the coast of Greece.

For her 85th birthday, she traipsed through the backcountry of Yellowstone National Park on snowshoes. She saw bald eagles and bison and hot springs and snowfall. I have pictures of her drinking vodka inside a Swiss ice cave, dogsledding in Lapland, riding an off-road Segway in Italy, tasting port in Portugal. She seems ageless.

I vividly picture our family photos in my mind. I was a tiny baby doll with barely any hair and a little blue bow taped to my head. I wore pretty, lacy dresses and bonnets at my mother's behest. There's a photo of her in a typical '60s knit dress holding me; her smile is big, her hair is big, and she is cradling me awkwardly down and to the side, showing me off.

We decorated my bicycle for the Fourth of July parade. I helped Mom make homemade ice cream in the old-school machine, where you put milk and cream and vanilla in the metal part, ice and rock salt in the outside part contained by wood slats and metal stays, and the plugged-in motor would churn for a few hours. Then Mom melted unsweetened chocolate with butter, sugar, vanilla, Karo corn syrup, and salt for her coveted chocolate sauce — we now call it Grandsue's famous — to pour on top of our ice cream. I liked it best served in pretty parfait glasses and topped with crushed pecans.

For birthday parties, we had friends over and Mom served homemade cake with vanilla bean ice cream. She threw themed parties for us where the kids dressed as animals, tea parties where we dressed like grown ladies, and then roller-skating parties as I got older. After my sister Sloan and I were off to college, Mom joined the Premier Club in Dallas. She took step aerobics classes almost daily. Now in Austin, she tracks her steps religiously. She knows exactly which routes around the Town Lake trail to walk one-and-a-half, two, and two-and-a-half miles from her apartment. Once my husband crossed paths with her while he was on a run; he reported that he was going to replace her porcelain coffee cup with one more appropriate for trail walking.

My sister Sloan and I became closer to our mother after our parents separated and divorced. When Mom had to move herself and my sister each year after I graduated, from Mockingbird to Southwestern to Abbott to Cole, she relocated her curated antique furniture and rugs, finest dishes, sterling silver, and crystal glasses, settling into each place and crafting a familiar home for my sister. It was strange to go to a different "home" each year after having lived in the same house from ages two to eighteen. The care she took with decorating helped me realize that home was wherever she was — like a little hermit crab, with a big smile and shell on her back filled with Colonial Williamsburg.

She hides well the signs that betray her age: the neck scar where she had four vertebrae fused; the long scar from an emergency hip replacement in Athens, Greece, only visible when she's wearing a cute bathing suit and hosting grill night at her apartment pool. She's a skillful entertainer, and we'll arrive to an outdoor table set with a tablecloth, napkins, silverware, wine, and flowers. She'll bring down trays with appetizers, marinated asparagus, steaks, and something vegetarian for

Top left: Youthful Grandsue in Greece, happiest when with her kids and grandkids.
Top right: Skiing with Mom at 85 and Sloan. Bottom: Grandsue sails the monohull at 86.

my sister. We bob in the pool while my husband grills, my brother-in-law provokes a political discussion, and we watch the wind ripple the surface of Ladybird Lake while the sun sets behind the clouds.

Though it's rare, we have talked about death. I picture Mom one day last winter after a walk together. I'm writing her a check for wallpaper (she has helped decorate our Colorado house), and she's smiling and walking in place to get more steps in while I finish a call. I hang up the phone and hand mom the check. I tell her that my colleagues and I have been talking about the Buddhist practice of keeping a fear journal. Every day you face your fears, so that they have less control of you. We all know we're going to die, so why spend time being afraid of it? Mom says, still stepping in place, "Sometimes I think it would just be nice and simple to go to sleep and not wake up." She's a woman of faith. I agree that sounds like a nice way to go, but I'm not ready for that any time soon.

All these memories swelled when Mom had a brief health scare after her 85th birthday. When she was in the hospital, I felt a strong urge to tell her that I never meant to hurt her feelings by finding my birth mother. My biological mother knew me for just under nine months, inside her body, and only moments after that. But my mother has loved and raised me for 57 years. There was never and will never be a comparison or a competition for who Mom is to me.

Mockingbird Lane

I grew up at 3628 Mockingbird Lane down the street from Southern Methodist University in Highland Park, which is its own municipality in the center of Dallas, Texas, and is known as "the Bubble." In many ways it was, especially economically and socially. My parents bought our house so I could go to Highland Park schools, which were independent. I was a scrawny kid my mom didn't want bussed to the other side of town. (A 1971 federal court order required Dallas Independent School District to remedy historical segregation and inequality by bussing students across town — ultimately a fraught and flawed effort.)

In HP, living in the bubble meant I went to reputable public schools with the wealthy kids, enjoying fancy athletic facilities along with the protection of the dedicated local police and fire departments. Bubble life helped buffer from the realities of the outside world. Because we lived on the busy street (a bit less safe), went to a small church (rather than the huge popular one in the neighborhood that also provided social opportunities), and didn't belong to a country club, sometimes I felt like I was just outside the bubble looking in.

The Mockingbird Lane house was built in 1917 — a lovely colonial style pier-and-beam house painted white with red trim. Though it had full panes of glass, my mother added plastic inserts that gave the appearance of each window having nine smaller panes to achieve a more traditional look. The inserts had to be removed to clean the windows — a small price to pay.

Our house was full of red, white, and blue wallpaper, freshly upholstered furniture, Oriental rugs, landscape paintings, and polished antique wooden furniture. We had a baby grand piano in the "piano room," which was a converted screened porch. I spent hours there from the time my feet dangled high above the pedals. From my earliest days, music had the power to move me and enable me to access rich emotions.

The wooden staircase with its curving banister divided the house in half, climbing up to the second floor opposite the front door. The staircase was the

With Sloan in matching outfits, ages 11 and 3.

backdrop for many photos with the cousins, us all dressed up, or with family friends in coordinated pajamas for extended family sleepovers. When I was older, I figured out how to sneak out by scaling the banister, skipping the third stair from the top, which creaked the loudest.

Every year, a week or two before Christmas Day, my parents would host a big Christmas party. The preparations took hours. Our shiny, antique wooden dining table was covered with food: a honey-baked ham, soft buttery rolls, mustard, and horseradish. Mom made olive cheeseballs, holiday punch in a clear crystal bowl, chocolatey Texas sheet cake, and filled sleigh-shaped baskets full of candy canes. Only at the Christmas party was I allowed to have a Schweppes Bitter Lemon — it was tart, bubbly, and made me feel adult. We strung fragrant evergreen garlands and lights on the table, weaving through the chandeliers, and twisting down the banister. We always had a fresh Christmas tree full of decorations and ornaments: homemade and travel souvenirs, shiny orbs, and holiday lights. Mom arranged the perfectly wrapped presents on the needlepoint tree skirt in anticipation of Christmas Day. I was a princess for a day, the kid in charge of the house, the games and toys upstairs, and any sweets the guests might receive. Kids from church, school, and of the employees at Dad's law firm received a decorated cookie or ornament.

The Dallas women were always dressed to the nines. They had big, wavy hair; fancy red, green, or gold dresses; heavy jewelry; and fur coats laid on an extra bed during the party. The men wore suits or slacks and sweaters since it got cold in December. I was dressed like a doll in red velvet, white tights, and black patent

Top left: Excited for my 5th birthday on Mockingbird Lane. Top right: All dressed up for a party; napping with pink rollers under the old fashioned hair dryer. Bottom left: Dressed up on the velvet couch in the living room on Mockingbird Lane; kneesocks pulled up high, leather buckle shoes. Bottom right: With Dad on the staircase that often was our photo backdrop.

leather shoes. My fine hair was straight as a board, but Mom would wet my hair and put it in pink foam rollers, and I'd nap on a fancy rug on the floor while the blow dryer dried my hair. This contraption consisted of a plug, cord, motor, and a hot air conveyance tube attached to a headpiece with an elastic edge like a shower cap. I looked like I was in an alien movie, tethered to the wall of the mother ship, receiving a brain infusion.

Each Christmas Eve, we cooked Ladybird Johnson's chili recipe for dinner, went to church, read a holiday story together, opened one present (always holiday pajamas, which we captured in action photos the next morning), and set out cookies and milk for Santa and oatmeal and carrots in the yard for the reindeer.

Top: Joyful with matching PJs Christmas morning. Bottom: Typical family photo on the staircase on Mockingbird Lane.

Christmas morning was full of anticipation. I woke up before sunrise, shook my parents awake, dashed down the stairs, and leapt into the living room — alone for my first eight years, then holding my little sister's hand. There, I saw presents piled high under the tree, and I searched for one small present wrapped in yellow ribbon tucked back in the branches (containing some candy, a little game, a stuffed animal). This one was from Santa Mouse, a character from a picture book we read annually. Santa's helper, Santa Mouse, fell out of the sleigh during a snowstorm but parachuted to safety using a present wrapped with yellow ribbon. Santa Mouse scrambled down a chimney, nestled into a child's Christmas tree near the top by a yellow light, and waited for Santa there. I always felt nervous anew each year for the tiny, frightened mouse. To my relief, he was rescued by Santa on Christmas Eve, which made the Christmas morning, yellow-wrapped find even better.

Santa always placed my biggest present of the year near the fireplace. After Santa's big present, I opened my stocking and tabulated the chocolate kisses, Life Savers, oranges, and Trident gum. Then we savored mom's homemade coffee cake loaded with cinnamon and butter. Sometimes one of our grandmothers, Gigi or Granny, joined us, and we all lingered around the tree, enjoying food, presents, and the warm glow of the fireplace.

I have continued many of these traditions with my children, plus our family friend Dave's boozy eggnog, which ferments for days. We double up on Christmas morning with my mom's coffee cake and my mother-in-law's cinnamon rolls. The air smells of baking spices and pine needles as holiday tunes play in the background. Our dogs get treats in their stockings and spend the rest of the day tearing up the wrapping paper.

Growing up in such a lovely home, surrounded by beauty and order, I sensed that things around me were under control. Things felt almost perfect, even dreamy. Looking back on these memories brings me a quiet comfort but also a desire to understand when things changed for me. Once my sons were born, I recreated the Santa Mouse tradition instinctively, gifting them the magic from my earliest days.

McLain Family sailing trip in the British Virgin Islands — I loved standing on the bow in the wind.

Going Outside

When I got home from elementary school, I'd have a snack and watch the after-school television specials, often about kids who kept a house key on a shoelace to let themselves in after school while their parents were still working. That was foreign to me. Mom prepared dinner, Dad would be home from work soon, and after homework and piano, I could play outside.

Our backyard was a big swath of grass lined with perimeter garden beds and a wooden fence. There was a swing set off to one side. I liked the swing, but I loved looking for crickets and beetles. I tried to get crickets to walk on a string tied across the top of a bucket, concocting a cricket circus. I liked the feel of holding a large zebra beetle with an ornate black and white shell and little antlers branching out of its head.

We had a tetherball game with a bright yellow ball tied to a pole with a rope. Near the tetherball pole was a nook under the garage stairs where the garden hose lived. There was a pan there to collect drips from the hose bib. To my delight, I found the drip pool teeming with tadpoles. Transfixed, I watched them transition from legless, tailed creatures, growing tiny amphibious limbs, then losing their tails and hopping away.

On summer evenings, to the pulsing trill of the cicada's song, I chased fireflies. I could only see them when they turned on their iridescent taillights. If I caught one, Mom found a glass jar and used the ice pick to poke a breathing hole in the metal lid. I added a few blades of grass, deposited the lightning bug, and watched it turn off and on like a yellow caution beacon.

I scoured tree trunks and the garage door frame for cicada shells. They were like crispy brown candy, a perfect mold of the cicadas' huge oval eyes, blocky head, segmented carapace, and folded wings — but split open right down the back to the tail, tiny claws clinging tightly to whatever foothold it used to emerge from the shell and fly away.

When the porch light went on at dusk, June bugs (scarab beetles) and daddy longlegs (cellar spiders) clung to the back screen door. My parents warned me not to touch the caterpillars with spiky fur called asps — they stung. But I knew other insects weren't dangerous. I plucked June bugs off the screen and let them traipse across my fingers with their sticky grip. The daddy longlegs had legs as thin as hair, and bodies the size of pencil erasers, but were as big as a silver dollar. They stopped walking to do eight-legged push-ups.

Near our front door, ivy twisted through the black wire railings. There I searched for chameleons (anoles). They changed color quickly and were easiest to spot when bright green. If you got too close, then they would set their feet and do lizard yoga, trying to look scary by inflating their fuchsia dewlaps under their chins. If I caught one by the tail, the tail would break off as the chameleon escaped, then grow back (or so I heard). Sometimes I found a praying mantis on a leaf in the backyard — elegant supermodels of the insect world, with their lanky legs and arms, hands folded reverently.

Dad bought me a microscope. I felt like a scientist when I took a drop of water from the pool by the hose, gingerly sandwiched it between two glass slides, positioned the sample under the aluminum clamps that held it to the viewing platform, turned on the light bulb underneath, and moved my eye to the eyepiece to see what wonders I could discover. I was captivated by my microscope — seeing life enlarged felt like learning a secret.

My curiosity about and love for nature started by exploring my own backyard. Remembering the hours I spent back there makes me appreciate that I found a career involving wildlife habitat and endangered species protection.

From my earliest days, adventures in nature, on the water, and in the mountains incited exhilaration and joy.

I grew up sailing on Texas lakes with my family. On Sundays after church, we packed lunch, filled the blue and white Igloo cooler with ice and sodas, and took off. We wore bathing suits, terry cloth cover-ups, sunscreen (SPF 4 or 8), and flip-flops.

Dad checked the outboard motor while Mom unwrapped the main sail, then stowed the tie-downs and ropes. From the cabin below deck, I handed up orange life jackets and seat cushions. With pride, I detached the slip ties that held us to the dock, tossed them onto the deck of the boat, and jumped on while we started floating backward out of the slip. Mom put up the bright blue sunshade, clipped the thin metal safety wires in place, raised the sails, and we launched out across the lake.

I loved the feeling of the wind in my hair and the splash of water on my legs, which I hung off the side of the boat. Mom and Dad took turns at the tiller, steering the boat and adjusting the sails. When my sister was old enough, we both posted up on the bow while we were sailing fast, and Mom or Dad would yell, "Coming about!" We'd lie flat, making sure the sail didn't knock us off the bow, then scooch over to the high side while the boat heeled the opposite way. We savored dropping anchor in a cove to jump off the bow. We tied a rope around a rectangular float to get towed behind the boat.

My sister and I took swimming lessons at the YMCA, so we were decent swimmers. Dad's idea of a good prank was to yell "man overboard" and grab one or both of us and hurl us off the boat while we were under sail. He'd toss us a life jacket and slowly tack around to pick us back up. We yelled at him, irked that he'd surprised us and threw us into the water unwillingly. Maybe it wasn't the best idea to toss children into a lake, but we were proud to pass our "man overboard" drills.

After a few hours, it was time to head in. I reveled in being the first one off the boat to help guide it into the slip and toss the lines to other passengers, who would secure the bow and stern to hold the boat in place. We lugged picnic baskets, the cooler, trash, and towels back to the car. The sun descended while the insects of dusk made a racket. We piled everything into the trunk, settled into the backseat, sunburned but satisfied, and fell asleep on the long drive home.

Some of my best memories of growing up were in the Colorado Rocky Mountains. Our family took road trips to Keystone in a boxy blue van with shag carpeting, captain's chairs, and a fold-down couch that also served as a bed. We stopped at a ski clothing warehouse in Amarillo that had good deals on new ski outfits for quickly growing girls. We always picked out a matching hat with a pompom (before helmets were commonly worn). Once we saw the evergreen trees and signs of snow lining the winding roads, we squinted our eyes to look for bighorn sheep high up on the rocks.

Skiing in a new outfit and pompom hat, 5th or 6th grade.

I became a good skier. I examined the snow-covered trees while riding up the chair lift. After unloading from the lift, I tightened my boots, checked the map, and headed off for fresh powder, tree runs, and small jumps. I earned my fitness and good balance from gymnastics. I tasted exhilaration when I sped around the moguls and felt a tingle of fear in my stomach.

After skiing, I took on sledding or ice skating on the frozen lake. At the end of middle school, my cousins and I styled our hair with the curling iron, put on our Gloria Vanderbilt jeans paired with a resort sweatshirt, and hung out at the pizza place, playing pinball and dropping quarters in the jukebox to play Foreigner and Journey.

During high school, we wore Sony Walkman cassette players with wired headphones tucked under our beanies and listened to Adam Ant, the Police, or U2 while racing down the hill. It was exciting to night ski, especially if we managed to get hold of Peppermint Schnapps to spike our hot chocolate. Drinking and skiing (at night, with no helmets) was a dangerous formula, but I soaked it up, invigorated. Spending time in high-mountain altitudes looking out over the landscape left me awestruck by the grandeur of nature, grateful I could experience it, and longing for more. To this day, I've worked to both protect the natural world and be able to provide similar outdoor experiences for my family.

Top: Last sail on *The Good Life* with Grandsue. Bottom: Early ski trip with Corbin and Beckett in New Mexico — before helmets.

Jane Sears at 20 — our matriarch.

Queen Bee

Jane Pringle Sears, my "Gigi," was my maternal grandmother and the matriarch of our family, as well as my namesake (Pringle is my second middle name). Gigi was a glamorous, world-traveling woman with a prideful, stubborn demeanor. Once, when she was in the hospital, I asked how she was doing. She replied, "Well, they say I'm being a bitch, so I must be fine." At such times, we referred to her as Queen Bee.

Gigi often mentioned that her father was superintendent of schools in Bowling Green, Ohio. There she took elocution classes and could recite a poem called "Little Rocket's Christmas" by Vandyke Brown, in its entirety, until her final years:

> ...And the only one who has heard her cry,
> Or, hearing, has felt his heartstrings stirred,
> Is Rocket — this youngster of coarser clay,
> This gamin, who never so much as heard
> The beautiful story of Him who lay
> In the manger of old on Christmas day!

Any time Gigi recited this poem, she spoke clearly, loudly, and commandingly. And she laughed in the same way.

My mom has often said that Gigi was bitter about not having finished college. Tom was her college boyfriend when a series of tragedies changed their trajectory. Tom was sailing with his little sister, Susan Jeanne, when they were caught in a storm. He tried to save her but couldn't, and she sadly drowned. Grandad went on to name his children to honor his sister's memory, my mom Sharon Sue and my aunt Jeanne. Though he honored his sister by passing on her name, the nomenclature kept the tragedy top of mind. Grandad also lost two other siblings in their youth. After Susan Jeanne's death, he moved to Ohio State for his master's degree in electrical engineering. He couldn't stand to go without Gigi, so she moved

Top: With my mom Sue, grandmother Jane (Gigi), great grandmother Mabel (Grammabe). Bottom: Grandad, me, Gigi, Dad, snowman — one of the only picures of my grandfather and my backyard and snow (rare in Dallas) in 1974.

with him before graduating from Bowling Green State and always regretted not finishing her degree.

After Grandad finished his master's degree, they moved to Texas for his work, which involved sales related to electrical grid systems. For a while, they lived in Houston, but apparently my mom was hanging out with the wrong crowd (including race car driver A.J. Foyt), so Grandad picked them up and moved them to Dallas. Mom met my dad when she was in high school, and he convinced her to go to UT Austin with him. After Dad's brief post-grad stint with the Navy in

San Francisco, they returned to Dallas, where Dad started his law career and Mom became a teacher. Granny, my father's mom, and Gigi were both nearby.

I can see Gigi's house on Regent Drive in my mind's eye from all the time I spent there growing up: a low-slung, ranch-style, brick house with big front and back yards and a garage accessed from the alley. The entrance was centered in the front of the house. Off the hallway through a door on the right was the combination piano/sitting room near the front bay window (where the Christmas tree would go) and the formal dining room. Her decorations were exotic: jade statues she obtained when she took a cruise to Asia, fancy glass barware, mirrored cabinets, and bar carts. My cousins and I listened to her stereo while lying on the soft shag carpet with our ears to the speakers.

The kitchen was galley style with a small pantry and shelving units separating the cooking space from the breakfast area. My favorite dish was Gigi's breakfast special: toast with butter, fried eggs, and bacon — all smashed together in a bowl. There was a corded telephone hanging from the wall in the breakfast area. I remember calling my aunt for permission to go see a movie using that phone. I twisted the thick plastic coil in my fingers and held the head-sized handset against my ear hoping for a yes. She thought the movie sounded ridiculous, but she did say yes, so Gigi took us cousins to see *Star Wars* in 1977.

Behind the breakfast area sat the laundry room, entered through swinging saloon-style doors. Continuing into the garage, two Chinese coins with holes in the center hung from the ceiling to windshield height so when Grandad and Gigi pulled their huge cars into the garage they stopped exactly when the coins touched their windshields.

The living room sofas were covered with rich floral fabrics. A brick, wood-burning fireplace was the room's centerpiece, flanked by brass fireplace tools. There was also a TV in one corner, which perpetually aired *The Lawrence Welk Show*, *Hee Haw*, or *I Love Lucy*. A sliding glass door led to the backyard, where the cousins climbed the fence, the tree, and the molded plastic fountain in the corner.

Aunt Jeanne and my cousins lived a couple blocks away from Gigi's house. I adored hanging out with them. Shannon was a year older than me, Stacey a year younger, and Robb three years younger. Sloan was born another four years after that. In summertime, we spent hours at Sparkman pool, where my cousins tanned and won races on the swim team. I visited, pale as a ghost, and preferred flipping

Sloan and I toasting grandmother Gigi's 99th birthday, 2013.

off the side of the pool. I was frequently sunburned, and back at Gigi's house I would slather aloe vera on my pink, hot skin.

When I was five, I remember trying to keep up with my cousins, hobbling down Gigi's alley wearing a plaster foot cast, with a rubber stopper sticking out of the bottom so I could walk on it. I acquired the cast after I fell out of a tree and broke my foot at Aunt Jeanne's house when my parents were out of town. Aunt Jeanne tried to make me laugh by smelling my stinky foot and pretending to feel faint. I screamed loudly — my foot was broken.

Using humor to leverage ourselves out of pain has always been a core characteristic of our family, especially Aunt Jeanne and her daughters. Even when Gigi turned ninety, my cousin Shannon gave her a copy of the erotic novel *Fifty Shades of Grey*, which she received with delight. Her gold key chain to her shiny Cadillac said: "Screw the Golden Years." She lived to be 100 and died in 2014. Good longevity genes! Too bad they're not mine.

Granny's House

When I went off to college in California, then to work in New York, Granny Esther would write me letters containing family news and updates about how her roses were doing. She thought she had nothing to say, but I still have her letters, pre-served in her pretty handwriting. As adults both living out of state, my sister and I would call Granny to check in. She would pick up the phone and say, "It's a beautiful day! What are you going to do with it?" My sister and I had that assertion and question tattooed on our left forearms.

Growing up, we went to Granny's house on Stanford Street on Wednesday nights when my parents had church choir. I picture her small stone house: peace rose bushes in front and back, concrete steps up to the front door, the alcove filled with books. She always greeted me with a smile and a hug, her cigarette-laced breath temporarily overpowering the other smells in her house (usually food).

I have many memories of being at Granny's without my sister, due to our age difference. I would explore the house, a charming single-story home with an attic. After the book-filled vestibule, I passed through a rounded archway into the living room. That room had heavy, colorful curtains, shag carpet, an oft-used fireplace, a rabbit-eared TV on a stand, turned up loud to game shows such as *The Price Is Right* or *The Newlywed Game*. Granny always sat on the "divan" (couch) against the wall by the archway that led into the dining room, reserved for family dinners and holidays. Next to her perch, the phone was plugged into the wall, its handset attached with a spiral cord. She constantly played solitaire. Her cigarettes and ashtrays were there — she was a chain smoker for as long as I can remember. She quickly plowed through books, checking mysteries and romance novels in and out of the local library.

Her kitchen was the lifeblood of her home — its heart center. The round laminate kitchen table had four chairs with shiny cushions and metal legs. Hanging from the ceiling was a tiny hummingbird, made with a straight pin for a beak, a pecan shell for a body, the wings made of whirligig seeds that spun down from the maple trees. The little bird was painted green and pink with a white belly and dangled from a pin in the ceiling by a dental floss thread. While Granny prepared dinner, I sat at the table with my homework. When she was cooking, the warmth spread through the house like a blanket. Granny always made a salad with iceberg lettuce, yellow onions, peeled tomatoes, and Wishbone Italian dressing tossed in a plastic bowl. There was a pile of slender green onions and a plate of dipping salt for appetizers. The porcelain stove and oven were on an interior wall at the home's core. A bright light shone straight down on her worn-in, cast-iron skillet. Her Spanish rice recipe was my favorite, heavy on the stewed tomatoes and fresh garlic.

Chocolate pie, round steak, baked apples with red hots and butter, pralines, divinity, oatmeal lace cookies, and, in her later years, lots of strawberry pizza and salmon croquettes were signature dishes. She died in 1992, but I have her recipes, written on index cards in pencil (probably a pencil engraved with "Texas Meatpackers" from her brother Archie's company) preserved in a baggie.

Granny made gorgeous chocolate pies. The crust was always crumbly and salty. The meringue was tall, with caramelized tips on the crest of each peak. The chocolatey interior was rich and warm when we arrived for dinner. She would take my little sister by the hand and lead her into the kitchen and plunge a finger deep into the pie. It wasn't for looking at, it was for enjoying!

I don't remember Granny ever complaining. She never mentioned the mastectomy she underwent to treat her breast cancer, though her flesh-colored bra insert sat in plain view in her bathroom, where it intrigued me as a child. Granny came from tough stock. She was not a big woman — she was no-nonsense. She was born around 1910 in Silsbee in far southeast Texas. She married Francis Eugene McLain, and they lived in Amarillo for a while, since the dry air was supposedly good for his asthma. He died in 1944 when my father, Frank E. McLain Jr. was just seven years old. Granny was only thirty-four when she lost her husband. She moved her children to Dallas to get better care for her daughter Jane, who had contracted polio. Jane loved to tell stories about Esther being a flapper, traveling to Cuba to gamble, always playing cards. She had an entire life I was not privy to.

Since my father grew up without a dad, it makes sense that he was like his mom: a survivor, a loner, intelligent, analytical, the salt-of-the-earth kind. He considered himself lucky because he was invited to a Boy Scout meeting in the neighborhood where he met Lon, who would become a part-time father figure to him. Lon was a lawyer, which inspired my father to take the same path, rather than

Top: Jane, Granny Esther, and my dad Frank in 1949. Bottom: Mom, me, and Granny Esther at my Christening.

continuing to work for Uncle Archie at the meatpacking plant where Granny also worked in accounting. I have been grateful for every job I've had — I never forget that I am one generation away from slaughterhouse work.

Every time I left her warm home, I hugged Granny tight, breathed in her smoky, garlicky, sweet smell, and felt the hard boundaries of her bra's infrastructure against my bony chest. Later when I visited her in the hospital, she looked like a foreign object: her eyes closed, her black-framed glasses removed, her hearing aids gone, her dentures taken out, leaving a concave space where her smile used to be. That person was a shell of my Granny, the thin empty outside case that remains after the nutty, meaty pecan is extracted. I held her hand and told her I loved her. She murmured something and squeezed my hand. Her hands were always so strong. I knew she loved me, and she knew I loved her.

With Granny Esther in 1988.

Just a couple weeks later, I didn't travel home from New York for her funeral. It was expensive, and I knew she wouldn't have wanted me to. She would've wanted me to answer her question: "It's a beautiful day; what are you going to do with it?" I think of her whenever I do the crossword, or cook Spanish rice, or bake oatmeal lace cookies, or read a saucy novel. I think of Granny Esther whenever I look at my arm. I can picture Granny in the kitchen. And I can smell the garlic sizzling in the cast-iron skillet.

Awkward, Diligent, and Determined

Dallas, 1979 – 1982

Middle school is an awkward, transitional time for most teens, and I was no exception.

In the early 1980s, I was likely to wear a plaid button-down shirt, corduroy skirt, ribbon barrettes, a gold and lapis add-a-bead necklace, argyle socks, and docksiders. It wasn't cool to carry a backpack, so I was always schlepping a fat stack of books down the halls.

Before school, students gathered on the gym bleachers until the bell rang for class. Though I'd gone to school with 25 percent of the kids since kindergarten at Armstrong Elementary, I wasn't sure where to sit due to the ever-shifting social order. One morning in sixth grade, I stood inside the doorway leaning against the heavy gym doors, waiting for the bell to ring so I could get to class. I had set down my burdensome book pile on the floor.

Then the bell rang just above my head — a brain-rattling, clanging metal bell. I bent down to pick up my books when a flood of zitty middle-schoolers swarmed the gym exit and knocked me down. I was trampled, my books strewn around the hall, my ribbon barrettes jostled out of my fine blonde hair, and I panicked. Next thing I knew, an eighth-grade boy (!) — a neighbor — yanked me up by one arm and set me on my feet out of danger. He was gone in a flash, as was the mob. I was left to gather my books, their brown paper book-covers ripped. I smoothed down my hair, made sure my clothes weren't torn, and stumbled to class — tardy. I felt beat down, small, and weak.

In contrast, I thrived at summer camp. I attended a Christian athletic camp in beautiful, wooded Missouri after seventh and eighth grade. We each chose a

Left: Class photo with retainer and grosgrain ribbon, 5th or 6th grade.
Right: Sloan and I playing in the backyard with our dog Mitzi on Mockingbird Lane.

major and a minor sport — gymnastics and dance for me. I did well in athletics, especially gymnastics. I was called "diligent" for the first time, and I accepted that with pride.

In the evenings, we had programs: skits by the counselors, singing by a bonfire, or testimonials by the camp founders. The camp founder's intertwining of Bible stories with the morality lessons that came after tales of his miscreant youth fascinated us middle schoolers. Whether I was captivated because he was a compelling speaker, a good preacher, or because he'd lived a racy life, I'm not sure. He taught us that every effort we made should be done in God's name.

The summer of 1982, I was excited to go back. When I arrived, the camp sound system blasted Survivor's "Eye of the Tiger." I worked hard at sports and methodically highlighted my Bible. I did gymnastics for God. I did blob for God! The blob was a huge plastic bladder filled with air, floating on the lake, tethered to a dock. One person jumped off the dock onto the blob and bounced another person up in the air to do tricks. I delighted in being the one launched because I could twist and flip before plunging into the water.

Later that summer, camp ended abruptly for me. I was called into the main office and was told that my best friend's mother had been killed. I was shocked. On the other end of the phone, my friend was sobbing and crying that she could not believe her mother was gone. My parents brought her with them when they picked me up.

The event was a shock to the community, but I don't recall any discussion at school, and I don't remember the funeral. Untimely death was not a proper topic to discuss in Highland Park in the 1980s. Everyone plugged along and kept up appearances, including me. My religious zeal quickly diminished. I'm not sure how my friend and her brother made it through the following days, weeks, or months. But when it came to years, my friend went to a great college, earned advanced degrees, and became a caring mother.

During one college summer, my friend and I went to see a movie called *Damage*. Tragedy struck the protagonist's life, and mayhem ensued. The final line of the movie was, "Damaged people are dangerous." Out loud, my friend blurted, "That's bullshit. One incident does not define your life." Certainly, that one incident alone has not defined her life. She's a therapist now, dedicated to helping people who've been through all kinds of suffering. She represents the choice each of us can make: Will we be defined by the challenges of our lives, or will we push against them and take control of defining ourselves?

I look back on my middle-school summers with nostalgia: the sweet innocence and physical exuberance, the unquestioning faith, then the startling slap of tragedy. I learned more from my friend's resilience and determination than I did from highlighting a Bible.

Part II: What We Seek

The high school years mark the change from being a child to becoming a young adult. We find agency in mobility and start to contemplate what we'll study to make a living. I found community, excitement for performing, and a taste of leadership through my high school drill team. I was happy and successful in school until my parents' divorce sideswiped me. Then I wanted to get out of Dallas. While listening to my internal voice to determine which life path to choose, the discomfort of my newly broken family pushed me away from my hometown.

I left Texas for California, restlessly seeking deep friendships, challenging academics, and liberating adventures. I left the country to study overseas, eager for broader perspectives. I sought identity and self-sufficiency when I moved to New York City and San Francisco to take my first shots at life in the real world. I wasn't thinking consciously about being adopted. But I nested wherever I lived, hanging pictures, posters, and tapestries. I tucked into a tiny, lofted storage space that became my bedroom. When we feel adrift, we seek home.

Highland Belles drill team lieutenant (junior year) or captain (senior year).

Most Ambitious

Dallas, 1982 – 1986

Freshman year of high school, after a mediocre semester on the track team, I was in the market for a new sport. Luckily, some senior girls had established a new drill team, an organized dance team that performed during halftime at football games. To audition, we had to learn and perform dances and high kicks in front of a panel of intimidating judges. I was overjoyed to make the team as one of a handful of freshmen.

I still have faded Park Cities People newspaper clippings that show a skinny me at practice in white tights, leg warmers, Keds tennis shoes, a white- and turquoise-striped leotard, and a bandana tied around my forehead to keep the sweat out of my thick mascara. We "Highland Belles" made a big splash in the community.

We had intensive summer practice and camps, then practiced twice a day during football season. I was thrilled when we got our formal field uniforms, navy with yellow gold trim and white fringe in a V at the chest and top of the legs. Officer uniforms were white, with yellow-gold trim and white fringe. We presented new dances each week and were invited to dance at community events. We practiced hard for precision and synchronicity; we strived to touch our knees to our noses with our high kicks. Once we started dancing and forcing ourselves to smile, we became one pulsing organism. I was hooked.

As a junior, I made lieutenant, meaning I wore the white uniform, danced in a five-girl line in front, and was responsible for a group of a dozen girls. I was expected to set an example both inside and outside the gym. Senior year, Coach Wheat surprised me by asking me to be the captain. I had never been given such a responsibility, and I was honored that she saw leadership potential in me. I worked hard at the job.

I thrived on competition. Twice I made the All-American drill team and was invited to perform in Mexico with girls from around the US. We appeared on *Hoy Mismo*, the Mexican equivalent of *The Today Show*. My three and a half years on the drill team challenged and anchored me. The leadership role, the discipline, the rigorous schedule, and the physical exercise gave me a strong foundation for juggling responsibilities thereafter. Being a Belle was my earliest experience of being in a group of founders. The Belles have become a well-funded, well-oiled machine, winning countless awards. In 2016, the charter members presented me with an Outstanding Alumna award for transferring the leadership skills I'd learned into a successful career as an entrepreneur.

I went through the normal transformations that occur in high school — fear, conformity, questioning, and finally, a little self-possession. The Park Cities comprise just under six square miles but exponentially more psychological and social real estate (thus the Bubble nickname). Fortunately, I found some true friends at Highland Park High School who were smart, interesting, and not obsessed with being the most popular girls in school. Like me, most of those friends went out of state for college.

From the ages of four to eighteen, I took private piano lessons. I was in a solid habit of practicing for about an hour a day during the week. That plus drill team kept me busy.

My piano teacher, Ms. Trudy, was a smiling woman with white hair and a gentle disposition. She taught lessons in her home. Once I arrived, Ms. Trudy allowed me ten minutes to catch up. Sharing the pressures of high school life was therapeutic. After we talked, I could relax into playing. Piano exposed me to talented historical composers, gorgeous pieces, a practice regimen, guts to perform, and the unplanned side effect of being a lightning-fast typist.

My mind expanded on a church volunteer trip to Haiti between my sophomore and junior years. Northridge Presbyterian Church took a group of medics, pharmacists, a dentist, church staff, and two teens — me, an incoming junior; another girl, an outgoing senior; and my mom. We spent a week at a modest Presbyterian property and did various volunteer activities. I remember one gathering where children and old people alike circled around me and touched my hair, which was very blonde — they wanted to see if the white color would rub off. The local people had so little, yet they were so kind to us.

Haiti was poor and the literacy rate was low. I was surprised to learn that people got their news on the radio. At night, the adults would sit together and talk about the day, and I'd listen. There were memorable stories about Jean-Claude "Baby Doc" Duvalier, who was the dictator in charge at the time, as well as his paramilitary force, and Vodou. Their discussions both mystified and scared me and gave me a newfound appreciation of democracy in the US.

Back at home, I paid close attention to the pro-democracy movement and the first democratically elected leader of Haiti, Jean-Bertrand Aristide, in 1991. People listened to the radio, knew they had a chance to vote for the first time, stood in line, and risked their lives for democracy. My visit to Haiti in 1984 solidified my adamant view that people should never take their right to vote for granted — my sense of justice took root.

When I first earned my driver's license, I inherited my Gigi's banana-yellow 1967 Plymouth convertible. I was too self-conscious to realize it was a cool car. When it caught fire due to a faulty ignition in front of Granny's house, my dad presented me with a surprise.

Dad walked in the back door of Granny's house. I was at the kitchen table handwriting my homework assignment with a bottle of liquid paper nearby. Granny was cooking dinner. Dad asked a leading question like, "What's in the driveway?" When I bolted out the back door and saw the low-to-the-ground, shiny hatchback, I was ecstatic. I didn't care how many miles it had on it or that Dad bought it at auction. I thought my social status would rise by driving my cool stick shift Mazda RX7, rather than the Plymouth Banana. In the refuge of my own car rather than Mom's, I was in control of the music and soaked it in. I began to listen to music intently, particularly artists who spoke out politically such as Sting and U2. My mobility signified the beginning of my independence.

My junior year of high school, my parents were adding on to our house on Mockingbird Lane, so we lived at Granny's house for several months. Mom oversaw the decorating. The back of the house was sliced off and expanded. Downstairs, we had a modernized kitchen and large living room with fireplace and floor-to-ceiling windows. Upstairs, there was my parents' new bedroom suite and bathroom complete with a cedar closet and a fireplace. I got my parents' former bedroom with a rebuilt bathroom and closet. We had a new swimming pool and backhouse accessed via covered walkway. It was exciting to move back into this beautifully decorated, fancy house.

Soon after we moved back in for my senior year, Dad started working late a lot. Sometimes I set the dinner table for the four of us, but my mom, sister, and I would end up eating while Dad's dinner sat waiting in the warming drawer. I was clueless and didn't speculate. Now, I dissuade my architect husband from including warming drawers in his designs.

Thanksgiving that year, after an intense drill team season, Dad asked me to sit down in the living room. I can picture him in the tall armchair, his back to the wood-paneled fireplace wall, the new pool visible through the window behind him. He wore business pants and a crisp white button-down shirt. I was sitting in my drill team clothes on the freshly upholstered, blue-and-white couch in the living room, the ornate Heriz rug between us. He plainly said he was moving out and divorcing my mom. I was shocked. I don't know if I yelled, or cried, or turned my back and stormed up the stairs. I can't recall saying anything to him — divorce was beyond the realm of possibilities I could imagine for our family, especially right after remodeling our home.

My memories get a bit jumbled around that time, but I decided I was no longer going to be the "perfect child." I was going to stop shaking a finger at the party crowd around me and see what everyone was talking about for myself. Friends took me to a Chinese restaurant where we knew they wouldn't ask for IDs, and we ordered nauseatingly sweet and highly alcoholic drinks. One friend had a fancy house with a pool and frequently absent parents, so that was often our chosen destination. Once, friends and I were busted on "minor in possession" charges, and I had to work overnight at a women's drunk tank. Fortunately, this was life before cell phones and social media, and we could make some bad decisions and stupid choices that are part of normal human development without being recorded on video or publicly shamed.

Despite these experiences, I was still high-achieving and compliant in school, a common expectation for Highland Park girls. I made the academic Top Ten in a class of around 350 students, piled up drill team accolades, and played a role in the senior musical (I was Cha Cha, the dancer, in *Grease*). According to

Left: Mom, Sloan, and I dressed up for Easter, 1986. Right: HPHS graduation ceremony.

the school newsletter, *The Bagpipe*, I received the embarrassing superlatives: Best Kisser, Tightest Jeans, and Most Ambitious (my friends were in charge).

In high school, I drove my beloved Mazda to drill-team practice before dawn and back home after dark. I kept working hard academically, dancing on drill team, and playing piano. But when I was driving around, I listened to Peter Gabriel, Madonna, The Fixx, Asia, and Yes. Music made me feel full of potential, vibrant, and I dreamed of being old enough to leave high school, Dallas, and my parents.

Sting's singing was transcendent — his high voice, his bass guitar, his jaw-dropping good looks in a red leather jacket — and I was rapt by his messages. His songs exposed me to the struggles of the world. In 1985's *The Dream of the Blue Turtles*, Sting's lyrics addressed economic issues in "We Work the Black Seam" and conveyed hope that "the Russians love their children, too." While I took Sting's music and lyrics to heart, my peers' obsession with fashion and flirtation seemed empty and superficial.

In the mid-1980s, it was common to apply to about five colleges. I submitted paper application materials to Duke, Georgetown, Stanford, Vanderbilt, and University of Virginia, and I was admitted to all except Georgetown. I believe I was accepted to Stanford because I responded honestly to the prompt, "Who would you like to spend the day with — living or deceased — and why?" Rather than yearning to be with George Washington, Jesus, or my grandfather, I wrote an unrestrained and heartfelt essay about preferring to spend the day with Sting, under the assumption that there was no way I would be admitted, so why not let it all hang out? I typed up that earnest and compelling essay on my mom's friend's typewriter.

When I received the acceptance letter, I fell down in surprise. I had never been to California. Early in high school, I visited the guidance counselor with my dad and when asked where I wanted to go to college, Dad answered for me: "Stanford." I laughed it off. When I told the family I was accepted, Granny went to the police station and told them if they didn't give her an old Stanford Street sign to send to college with me, they would find a little old lady in tennis shoes, wrench in hand, on top of the signpost at the corner of Stanford and Hillcrest where she'd lived for decades.

My final piano performance was a Senior Recital held at our home on Mockingbird Lane. My teacher and I worked on the pieces for a year. For the recital, Mom rented a second baby grand piano and had it installed on the back patio along with the baby grand piano we already had — a logistical feat. On the big day, the house looked beautiful. Mom was proud and printed programs to make it a special experience. I played several solo pieces, including the challenging "Fantasie-Impromptu" by Chopin. The finale was Kabalevsky's "Youth Concerto," which required both pianos. My teacher and I faced each other through the open crisscrossing lids of the two pianos. We communicated with facial expressions to stay in sync. It's a gorgeous piece, going from fast, loud, and bold to quiet and sweet. I felt like a star, expertly playing that piece on a beautiful day under the oak tree in my backyard, surrounded by family and friends.

Our HPHS graduation ceremony was held at SMU's Moody Coliseum. We wore shiny blue gowns and mortar boards over patterned dresses and pumps. I remember being happy to be done. I was also excited to head out for a big trip. My mom, sister, and I would fly to Hawaii and stay with family friends for a week before I joined the People to People Student Ambassador trip to East Asia. I was part of a select group of twenty students from Texas and California who traveled with two teachers as chaperones. We visited Korea, Japan, Taiwan, Hong Kong, and China, exposing me to vastly different cultures. In 1986, long before cell phones and the internet, the world felt so big. It made me eager to start life on my own in California.

All Right Now

Stanford University, California 1986 – 1988

When I showed up at my Stanford dorm called Otero in the Wilbur housing complex, I was greeted with cheers: "Welcome, Laura!" I had to tell them I go by my middle name, Ashley. I lugged in my boxes of stuff, including a typewriter I thought was high-tech because it had an automated carriage return. I was to share the first room on the first floor with a randomly matched roommate. I soon met Indu, a smiley coed from southern California. We hit it off immediately — we were both excited to start school, and we both loved to dance.

The students in Otero were interesting, nice, and talented. Before long, I stopped playing piano because I had an embarrassing experience when the Resident Fellow encouraged dormmates to play the piano. I decided to show off my toughest piece, only to be told by another freshman that they had played the same piece at the New York State Competition in fifth grade. Welcome to Stanford.

Our dorm consisted of three floors — girls on the first and third floors, a floor of boys on the second. Given the high number of young women, we always received invitations to parties on campus and in other dorms. We studied hard but also had fun. Otero hosted a three-level ocean waves/beach/undersea party, as well as an unforgettable heaven/purgatory/hell party. There weren't any police there, no one checked IDs, and nothing got out of hand. Stanford was a self-contained campus where few people had cars, so it was considered safe for nerdy kids to let loose every now and again.

I met my best friend Justine on her birthday that November. She lived down the hall. When I heard it was her birthday, I bought her a pair of earrings at a campus market and gave them to her. She was confused; she hardly knew me. I'm from Texas and was trained in good manners — which I made sure to pass on to my sons. Our friendship remains essential to me today. We connected in part because both our fathers had recently left our mothers, and we had some bones to pick about the "other women."

I fully embraced being a liberal arts "fuzzy" rather than a "techie" in 1980s Silicon Valley. My first big test was in my Great Works of Western Culture class. On test day, I opened a lined blue book and poured my heart out to the prompts on the page — I had loved the readings and let my emotion guide my answers. My hand started cramping, and my stomach hurt, but I kept writing, filling one blue book, then another. I left exhausted and eager for the teacher's response. When it came a week later, I took a deep breath and slowly opened the thin blue cover. To my surprise, my self-professed radical female professor had drawn a picture of a smiley face with a flip of hair and scrawled "not a dumb blonde" at the top of the page. I could have taken offense, but instead I beamed with pride! (For years, I joked I got into Stanford because they needed their quota of dumb-blonde Texans. I shouldn't have been so self-deprecating or flippant about quotas.)

I entered college knowing I wanted to study in Italy. I recall sitting in my Italian language classroom. Our teacher had wavy chestnut hair, red lips, and a gravelly voice that confirmed she was a smoker, as were all fancy Europeans. She launched right into speaking only Italian, and I clenched my jaw, nervous to talk. Thankfully, Professoressa initially had us speaking in unison. I flipped through the textbook to stare at the gorgeous Italian people, their clothes, the artwork, the scooters — I worked hard to excel in Italian so I would be admitted to the overseas studies program.

Intro to Art was difficult, requiring lots of memorization. In a stereotypical freshman moment, one Sunday morning, I stuffed my $42 *Story of Art* textbook into my laundry bag and headed into the basement. I started the wash, then couldn't find my book. I studied a different subject, then moved my laundry into the dryer and waited for the buzzer. When I pulled my laundry out and into the basket, bits of paper filled the sky like snowflakes. I had to start over with the laundry and repurchase the textbook. I was on my own for the first time, learning to balance newfound freedom, unprocessed feelings about my parents' divorce, and rigorous academics. I had growing up to do.

One RA knew I loved drill team in high school, and he encouraged me to try out for the Dollies — the five girls who dance at halftime of football games as part of the marching band (formally called the Leland Stanford Junior University Marching Band or LSJUMB). Tryouts were held in an auditorium, and we did our dances on the theater-lit stage. The audience was full of band members and former Dollies. They would hoot and holler to distract us. When it was my turn, the tryout

Performing as a Stanford Dollie with LSJUMB, 1987–1988.

music played on the PA system, and I proceeded through the standard dances. I sped along to the piece I'd choreographed, ending with a huge leap in the air landing in a split on the stage. The band members let out a groan imagining the pain of the jump split, followed by applause.

I was one of ten girls who made the short list. The final phase of the audition was attending a party in the "Band Shak" (the band had a whole vocabulary), interacting with band members so they could decide whether we would be any fun. We knew the five selected Dollies would be notified the next day. That meant getting dragged out of bed at dawn and taken to brunch at a diner in pajamas. That's when I met Dee, Anne, Shelly, and Patty — the four other Dollies I'd spend most of my time with over the next year. The nontraditional tryouts were a preview of the time I'd spend with the notorious LSJUMB. In 1987 and 1988, they recorded an album, so the five of us Dollies appeared on the album cover. *Rolling Stone* did an article on the band that year. We were excited to be in a famous magazine (despite the unflattering photo they selected). Starting that spring of my freshman year, I credit the Dollies with helping me get in shape and gain time management skills that would benefit me for years to come.

Me and Justine dressed as kelp for an undersea party at Stanford.

With the quarter system at Stanford, winter and spring quarters ran January through June, so by the time I returned to Dallas for the summer break, it was hard to find a job. I applied with Kelly Temporary Service, and they called me to work at a medical office as a temporary receptionist. The doctor's practice was in Oak Cliff, a south Dallas neighborhood with lower socioeconomic status than the Bubble. The job seemed simple enough: I would be the receptionist, taking phone messages, handling filing and other administrative tasks, while the original receptionist worked as the nurse, while the nurse was on medical leave. I borrowed Mom's clothes. I was timely and took care of my duties.

However, the job became uncomfortable. Once, the doctor called me into his office and pointed to a stack of Polaroid photos sitting on a bookshelf near me. I flipped through a couple and tried not to vomit, seeing naked bodies with hunks of flesh missing from a bacterial infection. Why was he showing me those photos? Did he think they would make me want to be a doctor? The images stuck with me like scenes from a horror movie. Either he enjoyed making me squirm, or he was truly unaware that what he was showing me was inappropriate. I don't recall telling my parents many details about that incident, but I swore I'd never go back to Dallas for the summer again.

For the second half of the summer, I returned to Stanford. The Dollies had to design our costumes and choreograph our dances for football season. Dollies lived with host families in posh Palo Alto, Atherton, or Menlo Park. Most "Dollie Families" volunteered to host because they had kids who might be inspired by

The Big Game: Stanford versus UC Berkeley.

having a college student in their home for a short time. My Dollie family was lovely, which was a nice rebound experience that deepened my love for California.

Sophomore year, I was happy to be rooming with Justine in Schiff, a new dorm with good dining facilities and parking. We had lofted beds above our desks. We listened to music — Justine introduced me to Joni Mitchell, Randy Travis, Lyle Lovett, The Smiths, and we both loved R.E.M., Talking Heads, and the Police. She played guitar and had a record player we listened to, along with the mixtapes we made with our boomboxes. We both had cars, and we always listened to our favorite music, whether we were driving to the city, the beach, or a concert in her hatchback or my Mazda RX7.

Football season was a blast. Game days started early and ended late. At half-time, it was a rush to dance on the field in front of thousands of people. Any time our team scored, we danced to Free's "All Right Now" (the Stanford fight song). It's hard for me to stand still when I hear the song on the radio even now.

Right before Thanksgiving in 1987, the Stanford band and Dollies performed in sparkly outfits at the "Big Game" (Stanford lost to our Berkeley rivals), and then I spent the holiday with Justine's family in San Francisco. I wasn't going home to Dallas because earlier that year, my mother and sister moved to Oxford, England. Mom was embarrassed to be separated from my dad and wanted to get away. She bravely packed their things and moved into a two-story cottage. My sister enjoyed Wychwood School, where she was instantly the best athlete. Mom studied classics, made church friends, and traveled.

Meanwhile, I dated a guy starting in the fall of sophomore year. He lived in a dorm called Cedro in Wilbur Hall, where, coincidentally, my future husband J.C. was living. The guys played rugby together (and both dated Ashleys). I felt cool when he gave me a scooter ride to the Band Shak or home from the stadium on game days when I was wearing my red-and-white Dollie uniform. Knowing I was one of only five girls wearing that uniform, I felt glamorous with my arms around his waist while he drove, tilting his head to the side to maintain the part in his hair.

At Christmas, Mom bought me a plane ticket to visit Oxford. Due to a misplaced passport, I was delayed by a day. Mom told me in no uncertain terms that I had to be there for a surprise on Saturday night. After food, a bath, and three hours of sleep, I was woken up and groggily put in a cab with my sister and her new school friend. As we drove for an hour, my sister gradually revealed our destination with hand-made clues. As soon as I saw the roadway exit for Wembley Stadium, I knew we were going to a concert. When she told me it was Sting, I was beside myself.

We had a sweet Christmas holiday. We ate Christmas pudding, heard concerts at churches, traveled to Wales, and celebrated with a tiny tree and my sister's long, skinny field hockey socks as stockings. Other than Mom accidentally singeing off some facial hair in a gas stove mishap, she created a positive and memorable experience for herself and my sister, which I was happy to briefly witness, at a time when Mom otherwise felt bereft.

After finishing sophomore year and the Dollie gig, I was accepted to the Stanford-in-Oxford summer session on Comparative Legal Systems of Britain and the US focusing on Human Rights and Civil Rights. Ironically, my mother and sister would no longer be living in Oxford that summer, but my boyfriend would be in London. I was admitted to the Stanford-in-Florence program for the fall, fulfilling one of the first dreams I had for my college career. I was proud and eager to spend half a year overseas.

Working on My Worldview

Oxford, England; Florence, Italy; Washington, D.C.; Stanford, California; 1988 – 1989

Spring quarter wrapped up, and I headed to Oxford. Our student group arrived at Heathrow and started collecting our bags. I stepped away to use the bathroom. When I got back, my whole group was gone! My bags were also gone, and I had nothing with me — not even my wallet. I had no way to call the Stanford Center in Oxford. The person at the information kiosk directed me to the bus terminal where I was told which bus to board. In my jet-lagged daze, I climbed the steps, said, "Excuse me, I'm an American student heading for Oxford, but my group left me. Would anyone loan me the money for a ticket, and I can pay you back?" Thankfully someone did just that.

When I arrived at Stanford-in-Oxford's center on High Street, the first adult I saw said, "Oh, there you are. We wondered what happened." What a start.

The center was a collection of several apartments connected with stairways and hallways, like a rabbit warren. I had a single room and settled in. It turned out to be both private and lonely.

Our courses were taught by Stanford law professors, plus one tutorial with an Oxford Don (a tutor, lecturer, or professor at traditional universities in England). We studied and compared the legal systems in Britain and the US, including approaches to race and sex discrimination. Another course focused on human rights, which I felt strongly about in part because the *Human Rights Now!* tour headlined by Sting was in the news. At the High Street center we studied a lot, ate scones, and drank tea. I took on the responsibility of cleaning one of the center's kitchens, which proved to be a chore when living with college kids not used to feeding or cleaning up after themselves. But I earned extra cash, which I had been worrying about since my parents' separation.

We had wonderful field trips visiting the Bodleian Library, seeing Christ-church Cathedral, and punting on the Thames. I spent several weekends in London and took short trips with my boyfriend's family to the horse races, where we drank Pimm's cups and admired the women's hats with fascinators (the feathery or flowery attachments). We drank lager with Rose's lime juice, or a Half and Half (Guinness and lager).

Since my Dollie friend Anne would be my roommate in Florence for fall semester, she joined me in England. We set out with our Eurail passes for adventures in Germany, Austria, Switzerland, and Spain. We traveled on a shoestring budget. We spent the night in a German train station because we didn't think we could afford the taxi cabs, not understanding that most German cars were Mercedes. We climbed up a mountain in Austria while the other travelers hauling around *Let's Go: Europe* (the preferred budget travel guide) had ridden the chair lift to the top. Anne refused to spend money on a drink when we made it to the peak. We were famished when we got to the bottom of the mountain, so I pulled out my dad's emergency American Express card, and we ate a big dinner before collapsing into dorm-style beds.

Our last night in Spain, we used our last pesetas to buy and split a bocadilla de patatas. We were horrified when the potato patty fell out of the sandwich onto the floor. Like feral animals, we snatched it up, wiped off the cigarette butts and dirt, stuffed it back between the buns, and ate it anyway. I had started to become aware of the need to pursue financial independence, watching Mom working in earnest as a decorator after her separation from Dad. Anne and I have been close friends for a long time, but only recently did I fully appreciate that she was a "FLI" or first-generation, low-income student who had come from a challenging family upbringing.

Before I left California, I secured a job to be the au pair for two children whose mother was leading a walking tour of Tuscany before teaching an Urban Studies course for Stanford-in-Florence in the fall. Anne traveled with other friends for the two weeks before classes started while I was working. I learned my way around Florence while my charges were in school (third and fifth grades). For several hours a day, before cell phones or the Euro (we used the colorful Italian currency, Lira), I spent hours wandering through the narrow stone streets, practicing the language, studying the art (Caravaggio) and sculpture (Donatello), imagining life in the Middle Ages and Renaissance. I tasted squares of pizza and cups of mouth-watering gelato. My language skills improved quickly. I met the boys' school bus, made dinner, oversaw homework and bath time, then let them read to me about paleontology or Pompeii.

With Anne, my roommate in Italy, in Florence.

Once the au pair job was up and classes started, Anne and I were roommates. Our host parents were Franco and Salvatrice. Their daughter and son-in-law from Sardinia lived in the home, too. They were great cooks and ran a gastronomia (a deli), while their son Valte had a restaurant called Acqu'al Due, which was listed in all the guidebooks because you could order the assaggi, which means tastes — a great way to try a variety of local pasta dishes. Some nights, Anne and I ate too much at home and couldn't get out of bed to go out with the other students after dinner.

Each day, I took the crowded bus back and forth between our host family's home and the Stanford Center, crossing the famous, shop-lined Ponte Vecchio. In 1988, we relied on centralized pay phones and either rode the bus or walked everywhere. We used desktop computers only at the Center, facing the Arno River. My Italian, Structure of the City, and Studio Art classes were held at the Center, while Art History — taught by a curator from the Uffizi Galleries — was held inside various museums and churches around town.

Visiting Santa Maria Novella and Santa Croce churches to study the frescoes painted directly on the walls was an unparalleled way to learn. We stood in the musty-smelling, cool, damp churches with sunlight filtering through stained-glass windows, spilling onto the walls and floor. Our professor explained how the plaster was applied to the walls and painted quickly before it dried. Masters worked with apprentices to pass along their skills. We learned to appreciate painters from the 1300s, such as Cimabue and Giotto, who came before the High Renaissance painters Leonardo da Vinci and Michelangelo. This art could not be transported and had to be seen in its original setting.

Though I was not artistic and had little skill, I enjoyed being creative in such an art-filled city in my Studio Art class. The piece I made was a watercolor — mediocre as a piece of art, but meaningful. I had painted a male figure in one top corner and a female figure in the other. They moved toward each other, then danced in the middle, separated away from each other, and ended up apart, at opposite corners of the bottom of the painting. With distance and time to reflect, I knew the connection with my boyfriend was weakening. I feared breaking up but also feared commitment after my parents' challenges.

In October, we voted with absentee ballots in the 1988 US presidential election between George H.W. Bush and Michael Dukakis. I voted for Dukakis and have been a Democrat focused on the goals of justice and equity for all ever since. By late November, to counteract Thanksgiving nostalgia, our Center chef, Settimo, spatchcocked a large bird to roast in the tiny oven. I can still picture his big smile as he carried the steaming bird to our communal dining room. It smelled wonderfully of sage and oregano, despite being flat as roadkill.

Winter quarter, I lived in Okada dorm back in the Wilbur complex and worked at the Center for Reliable Computing making photocopies of handouts covered with Xs and Os. In a dark, cluttered room full of machines, I checked the professor's email account and printed out his messages on z-folded paper with perforations between sheets and printer guide holes on the sides. I had no interest in this new "computer science," and soon after, I officially declared my American Studies major, which combined my interests in literature, history, and political science.

In a confusing turn of events, my dad had come back home to give his marriage to my mother one more try. I missed most of it, except a spring ski trip to Colorado that took place over Easter — Mom hid plastic Easter eggs full of coins for me and my sister in the condo we rented. She was trying to recreate simpler times and traditions, but I felt ridiculous rushing around to find the eggs, pretending as if nothing about our family had changed. Even plastic eggs wear out, and mismatched halves don't reliably fit together. Time was suspended; I was holding my breath.

Since I had been taking classes for six straight quarters, I took spring quarter off but stayed on campus and worked. I lived with a friend from the Florence program in Kinscote, which was an "off-campus" house right in the middle of campus. We slept on futons on the floor but didn't care because the location was ideal. I found a job assisting an English professor who was doing research on Christopher Marlowe, a contemporary of Shakespeare. I worked shifts at the campus Coffee House, wearing my LSJUMB bucket hat and making vanilla nut coffee and California club sandwiches.

Once during that spring, Justine and I stayed after hours at the Coffee House, which was managed by a friend of ours. He filled a pitcher with a mix of beers, which we drank while we laughed and told stories. We decided to climb the Stanford Dish, an undeveloped hiking area in the foothills that houses a huge radio transmitter. We were lying in the grass watching the sun come up when then-President (of Stanford) Donald Kennedy went jogging by. Fortunately, he didn't stop.

In May, the Grateful Dead played at Frost Amphitheater. The nomadic "Deadheads" filled the eucalyptus groves for the weekend. They created a small woodland city with painted VW bugs and vans, campers, and pop-up markets with tie-dyed t-shirts and Baja-style surfer hoodies. Everything smelled like patchouli and eucalyptus. I attended the concert with friends. When the Grateful Dead left for their next destination, the whole Deadhead village picked up and moved along with them. I feel lucky to have glimpsed that cultural phenomenon. Nowadays, outside the same eucalyptus groves, there are lines of worn-out RVs stationed along blocks bordering the campus. Only now, the people who live there are workers who can't afford to live anywhere else nearby.

My boyfriend and I tried to reconnect, but our romance was tepid. We carried on for a while, both of us avoiding the inevitable. I turned my energy toward finding a summer job in another city.

The previous summer of 1988 was known for the huge international *Human Rights Now!* tour, showcasing forty years of the *Universal Declaration of Human Rights*. Amnesty International was the beneficiary, and the Reebok Foundation was a key grantor. Sting, Peter Gabriel, and Tracy Chapman were among the headliners who brought international attention to human rights abuse. For this reason, my dream job in 1989 was to be an intern at Amnesty International in Washington, D.C. Fortunately, I was selected, and my parents agreed to cover my expenses so I could take the unpaid opportunity. I roomed with Stanford girls in Georgetown University housing; we were all working on or near Capitol Hill.

I commuted on the bus to Amnesty's offices. Our group of five interns were each assigned to a government program officer (GPO) for a certain geographic

In D.C. during a summer internship at Amnesty International, 1989.

region. My supervisor was the GPO for Asian Affairs. I started on a Friday. The next weekend, on June 4, 1989, the Tiananmen Square Massacre occurred — a violent military suppression of pro-democracy demonstrations throughout China, especially in Beijing. Immediately, the phone started ringing at Amnesty because people wanted to know if the organization could help find missing persons or help Chinese students in the US secure extended visas.

I spent hours clipping articles out of daily newspapers that covered the event, pasting them to standard paper, photocopying, and circulating them through the office, I was brought in to take notes when a Chinese dissident came for a sit-down meeting to recall their experiences of the event to Amnesty staff members.

Along with the democracy crackdown, the Chinese leadership stopped renewing J-1 visas, making it difficult for Chinese students to complete their studies in the US. One day, I received a call from an intern for the US Congressional Representative Mickey Leland, from Houston, Texas. Leland had created a group called Students for Students, and he had penned a bill trying to extend J-1 visas for Chinese students living and studying in the US.

On behalf of Students for Students, my Texas friend and I circulated invitations to other Congressional interns, encouraging them to attend a rally at the Capitol to gain visibility for our cause. Many interns and a couple members of the press attended the rally, and I was introduced to Congressman Leland there. We believed showing up for justice made a difference.

Meanwhile, my boyfriend and I officially broke up. I felt free. I'd met a Maryland guy who was looking for trouble, or fun, or both. When I wasn't working passionately on human rights issues that summer, I was having a proper summer fling and not worrying about the future. I recognized I was desirable, but I didn't owe anything to a guy; I could control what I gave and got from a relationship. Both the breakup of a young but serious relationship and the low-stakes fling prepared me for a mature and healthy future relationship.

When my internship ended, I stayed with high school friends for a few days in Martha's Vineyard. It wasn't a great trip: my friends were mostly working; I was stuck in a bed with biting bed bugs; and I got a call from my organizer friend that his boss, Mickey Leland, had died in a plane crash in Ethiopia.

Senior year, Justine and I were living in Kairos house, my favorite residence at Stanford. Kairos means the right critical moment. Kairos was a self-op, meaning we all pitched in to cook and clean, and we employed a student as house manager. J.C. was living in the Sigma Chi house at the time, just down the street. While walking to or from class one day, I distinctly recall seeing J.C. ride by in a jean jacket and green, high-top tennis shoes, on a hand-painted, multi-colored bicycle. He was wearing a hat.

Today, there is an environmental science internship program through the Texas Commission on Environmental Quality in Mickey Leland's name. Once I became an employer, I received several resumes a year from graduates of the program; I always took a moment to appreciate Leland's work for democracy.

Last Dollie performance at Stanford graduation.

Charmed and Irreverent

Stanford, California; 1989 – 1990

Fall was beautiful at Stanford. Football season was always fun, and games were well-attended. Sitting in the student section, I saw a rowdy group of guys, many of whom I knew. They were Sigma Chi frat boys, and I ran into J.C. He said: "I sold the shirt off my back!" He had made T-shirts with a dog wearing a Stanford pennant that said "Dog Cal" relieving itself on a hydrant labeled "Cal." He told me he'd gotten in trouble for selling outside the stadium without a vendor's license. I was amused by his entrepreneurial spirit and found his levity appealing.

Justine decided to head back to the dorm. J.C. said, "Who wants to go swimming?" It was hot, we were all sweaty, and I knew a lifeguard at the pool. I agreed, and J.C. and I set off to the university pool and plunged in fully clothed. We started trolling the tailgaters where alumni would set up drinks and grills to keep the party going. J.C. said, "Let's pretend we're married and hit the tailgaters." I thought, *Why would we pretend to be married?* I suggested we go back to Kairos where we had access to the kitchen, and I could make food.

While I prepped the nachos piled high with beans, cheese, sour cream, jalapeños, and onions, J.C. was busy juggling oranges and making me smile. Not yet knowing that J.C. had food allergies and aversions, I felt bad when he didn't eat much, then admitted he didn't like some ingredients.

Kairos was having a party that night, so I said he could go up to our room and hang out while I prepared for it. When I got back to the room, J.C. had spent the time cutting out paper dolls from a sheet of computer paper (which I preferred over the self-serious guys I dated around that time). I was charmed. J.C. was fun.

J.C. and I had back-to-back classes in one lecture hall. He had poli-sci after I had history. Somehow, we figured out where to sit in the lecture hall that had space for books under the long wooden tables we used for writing. We started leaving notes for each other between classes. This guy was clever and romantic. He came looking for me after the Loma Prieta earthquake in October. By Thanksgiving, we were dating.

I spent my senior year Thanksgiving at Justine's house in San Francisco again. I remember Justine telling me she was annoyed because her grandmother wanted her to wear more makeup. This unimportant conversation is seared in my memory because soon after, I called home to say Happy Thanksgiving. Since Dad was back, I assumed they would be cooking or at my grandmother's house. My mother answered the phone and in a low, zombie-like voice, she said, "He's gone again." I told her I was sorry. I was shocked. Dad had left our family again. Years later, Dad said he had given it one more try, and it confirmed he did not want to be married to her anymore.

I proceeded to eat and drink a lot that Thanksgiving, commiserating with Justine. I was relieved to be with her family, especially her strong mother Checka, grandmother Dita, and sister Jennifer. For Christmas, my mother, sister, and I traveled to Santa Fe to be away for the holiday, since being at home was too sad. When I returned to Stanford, J.C. had made me several pairs of earrings using his mother's African bead collection from when they lived in Côte d'Ivoire in the '70s, foreshadowing his design career and generosity.

J.C. and I both had birthdays in January. He received a pile of presents from his parents; I thought his mom might be overbearing. It turns out she is generous and loves to spoil her sons. For decades now, J.C.'s parents' solid relationship has been a counterweight to my parents' instability. J.C. and I share confidence about the potential strength of marriage alongside its fragility.

Winter quarter senior year was my last academic quarter. I took Introduction to Computers in which we taught Karel the Robot to jerkily move down a two-dimensional hill. I much preferred a class called Plath, Sexton, and Rich by biographer Diane Middlebrook; the feminist writings we discussed inspired me. I took an American Studies senior seminar that asked the question, "Is there an American national character?" I found that question both daunting and intriguing. I enjoyed arguing for my perspective. It centered on free speech, democracy, and diversity. I read a lot of Black women writers, many from the South. Their stories were rich — deep, difficult, unfair, and strong. I loved Alice Walker, Toni Morrison, and Zora Neale Hurston. I was drawn to their voices because I had not heard them before; where I grew up, the curriculum didn't represent them. My sense of justice and injustice deepened. I felt farther from my Highland Park upbringing than ever

— through my young eyes I saw righteous attitudes, conspicuous consumption, racial prejudice, and sexism.

My professor Jack Rakove influenced me during my Stanford education. He taught several courses I took, including a hefty senior seminar. He wrote my recommendation to be admitted to graduate school. When he was in Austin for a conference at the University of Texas at Austin, we had breakfast. He distinctly recalled telling me to stop apologizing for my opinions during class discussions. I had a self-defeating habit of starting any point with, "Sorry, but I think . . ." Though I don't remember that conversation exactly, I was buoyed that he did. Why would he remember one insecure student? Sometime between college and my career, I became an extroverted and talkative person, wanting to connect with others.

What I was learning and where I was living made me critical about where I grew up. In retrospect, I see that it was hard to separate my judgment about Highland Park from my judgments about my parents or how I felt about myself. Through his choice to leave Mom, Dad showed me that her efforts trying to be the perfect wife — in church, in the PTA, in the home, in the community, among the lawyer's wives, or on the symphony board — did not equate to the love or affection he needed. Instead, he chose someone who only cared about him. That choice was painful for Mom, my sister, and me. I felt angry and wanted Dad to explain himself and apologize to all of us. I also wanted Mom to be stronger and to not care so much about what Dad (or the community) thought. At the time, I focused on what Dad had done to Mom. It took me years to understand the impact of him also leaving me.

Looking back, I realize he never told me I couldn't be something academically, professionally, or otherwise. He never told me I couldn't have power in the world, or that I should or shouldn't marry. He did tell me, "Win a few, lose a lot," for as long as I can remember. It sounds like a dark view, but he always said it with a chuckle. For him, it meant you have to let defeats roll off your back. They shouldn't consume too much of your energy. I took his advice as a personal challenge — and ultimately benefited from it because it led to my deep desire to succeed.

I finished classes to complete my American Studies major after winter quarter, so I didn't take classes during spring of senior year. Fortunately, I was able to stay in Kairos house. I went to the campus resource center to look through binders with flyers and information about job opportunities. I took a writing course at Fort Mason in San Francisco and volunteered at California Lawyers for the Arts. Spring quarter went by quickly.

June arrived, and it was time for graduation. My mom, sister, Aunt Jeanne, and cousins Shannon and Stacey all came to San Francisco. We had a great time celebrating. Justine asked where I'd been hiding these women who were so much fun. We went to a lovely party hosted by Justine's family at her grandparents' home. We explored the city, and Mom relived her time in San Francisco in the early 1960s, not far from Haight-Ashbury. Back then, Dad was assigned to Treasure Island and worked as a lawyer for the Navy. They would go sailing on a beautiful teak boat some weekends, and Dad acted as an extra in the San Francisco opera. Mom told those stories as we walked through the hilly streets.

Then, as we were starting to trudge up a steep North Beach hill, Mom in the lead, two people appeared on the crest of the hill — a couple in matching red windbreakers. It was Dad and his new wife, whom he married a month before. My cousins and I promptly pushed Mom into the nearest bar and ordered a bottle of white wine. She cried and shook, and we all tried to let her sink into that moment, until she could find her way out of it, so we could focus on my graduation.

The women in my family use humor to survive. Even at that moment of emotional turbulence, someone made a comment, and we ended up laughing, mixing those tears with sad ones. My mom's side of the family has endured a lot of pain. But they — we — always pick ourselves up with a toast and a round of laughter. Sometimes we do this to a fault, when we should probably more deeply explore the bad or hurtful feelings. That weekend, I was grateful for my family's trademark resilient humor.

The next day, I rode my bike into Palo Alto to meet Dad at a coffee shop. I told him how angry he'd made me the day before. He laughed and said how funny he thought it was running into us. He truly thought I needed to lighten up about it, and it frustrated me. He acted insensitively, bringing his new wife to San Francisco for my graduation. In contrast to Aunt Jeanne and the cousins lifting Mom out of her pain with laughter, I reprimanded Dad for thinking it was funny because it was at her expense.

I received my degree in American Studies. The Dollies wore our uniforms under our graduation robes and danced one last time to "All Right Now" on the graduation stage in Stanford Stadium. It was the end of an era. I have lots of photos of my sunburned face, blonde hair, heavy mascara, and a big smile despite the stressors.

During the graduation ceremony, the convocation speaker said something that stuck with me: Be irreverent. It was surprising to hear in that setting, from someone who was blessing us to go out into the world after university. I was excited. Question authority; don't blindly follow the rules; have a little doubt; don't always do what's expected of you. I reflected that I had found some of myself in college, and I liked it. Rather than the Dallas sorority girl path, I chose the hippie co-op route and embraced it. I followed what felt like nature and rejected nurture.

At a graduation dinner, Mom presented me with a card. In it, she wrote that when I was planning to study overseas, my father said he didn't have the money to cover my costs. My mother applied for an emergency student loan so I could stay in school. Her gift to me was that she had saved up the money she received from Dad, plus her new interior decorating business, and paid back that $10,000 loan. That was quite a sign of strength. I am grateful my parents paid for my undergraduate education. I know that is a rare privilege. Other than a few short breaks, I worked continuously since that kitchen-cleaning job in Oxford. Money and fear of scarcity drove my motivation for years afterward.

One of my last memories at Stanford was being in J.C.'s room. One roommate had been in my freshman dorm. When J.C. and I were wondering how to say goodbye to everyone, our friend said, "Dude — it's not about the goodbye." He reminded us that it's about all the time we had together before the goodbye. We agreed and let go of leaving with a grand flourish.

It was time to join the real world.

My second job after college: Program Assistant for the NRDC's Coastal Program.

If I Can Make It There...

New York City, 1990 – 1993

In 1990, students had to find jobs by going to the career placement office at Stanford and leafing through binders of brochures and job descriptions. To apply, we copied down the contact information and job reference, then mailed off carefully crafted cover letters with our resumes, hoping for a positive response. New York rose to the top of my location list because I knew J.C. was applying to Mitsubishi International Corporation's program for Japanese speakers, and Justine was pursuing nonprofit work there. I had two interviews for legal assistant jobs — one for a Midtown Manhattan law firm where I would be one of eight people, and the other at the Lawyers Committee for Human Rights where I would be one of two people for a two-year commitment. I took the corporate job at Debevoise & Plimpton because I wanted a social life and better pay, plus working as one of two young people for two years seemed like a lifetime in a social desert. I would start in the fall. J.C., Justine, and I received job offers in New York within twenty-four hours of one another, and we all decided to accept and move to the Big City.

After graduation, I went home to Dallas to pack up my things, since we were selling the house I had lived in since I was two years old. I was more ready to get on with my life in New York than I was sad to move away from Mockingbird Lane. That happy, family-of-four life was over. I shopped for work-appropriate outfits, including dresses, colored pantyhose, and a warm coat for the New York winters. I then flew with my things to Vienna, Virginia, where J.C.'s family lived.

J.C. and his parents had kindly invited me to stay, but since we weren't engaged, we weren't allowed to share a bedroom. I spent two weeks in the damp-but-furnished basement, where my acne and rosacea protested loudly. I wrote pages in my diary about "gacky face." Thankfully, just before our job start dates in New York, we visited family friends at a South Carolina beach. The salt water cleared my skin, and I moved into my apartment with more confidence.

We drove to New York in a U-Haul with the heavy platform bed J.C. had built for himself, along with the few belongings I had brought. I shared an Upper

West Side apartment with childhood friends and a friend-of-a-friend from Dallas. Columbus at 95th Street was New York for beginners: We had a door man, laundry in the building, and a gym. J.C. and his two roommates lived a few floors up from us. My dad joked, "Wow, in a city of eight million people, what are the chances?" Eager to appear grown up, J.C. and I did laundry and subway commutes together.

That first year, we each found our way in our jobs and hung out with new friends and Stanford buddies on the weekends. At first, Sunday nights were for the week's grocery and outfit planning and Monday prep nerves. But Justine told us, "Sunday should be its own day!" It's been our motto ever since. On cold days, we'd get spicy noodles from Ollie's or catch a foreign language movie at Lincoln Center theater.

Though I enjoyed my legal assistant coworkers at Debevoise & Plimpton, my days were filled with page-checking contractual documents on heavy paper for corporate transactions. I worked late nights due to the firm associates' schedules. I took a car service home with a $25 dinner voucher if I had to work until 8 pm. Back then, $25 covered a hearty pasta meal that would feed me at least through lunch the next day. I was sure the associates killed time until they could do the same, which meant twelve-hour days. I watched the city from the backseat car window, marveling at the garbage trucks, delivery vans, medical and transportation workers starting their workday in the dark of night. I didn't complain because it was my first full-time, post-college job, and I was making good money. I had some rent support from my parents but knew I needed to be self-sufficient. I was building up my resources, navigating the subway and the teeming commuters and tourists. And I was determined to succeed.

There were bright moments of culture. In Central Park, we saw Denzel Washington play Richard III for free. We attended Paul Simon's free concert there in August 1991 among more than 48,500 attendees (the rumor was half a million people). That felt blissful — moved by the music, in communion with the peaceful throngs. I can't imagine such a gathering today without SWAT teams and camera drones. When J.C.'s family came to visit, we ate big, family-style Italian meals at Carmine's on Broadway and 90th, which smelled of garlic and tomato sauce and sounded loud with clanking dishes and boisterous servers.

I mentioned to one of my colleagues that I wasn't sure about applying to law school (the assumed path for those of us working as legal assistants). He asked if I liked adversarial situations; I gave an emphatic no — I spent my time avoiding them. He counseled that law school might not be the best path. I embraced being irreverent when I left my first job at the corporate law firm to focus more on environmental causes.

Though I'd spent that fulfilling summer at Amnesty International working on human rights issues, I realized that field would be soul-crushing as a career. I volunteered a few hours a week at the Lawyers Committee for Human Rights, but I couldn't focus every day on extra-judicial killings, torture, and suppression of free speech. A colleague suggested I look more broadly at the not-for-profit sector for organizations working on environmental issues: water quality, air quality, endangered species protection, etc. After some research, I got excited. I applied to job postings at the Sierra Club and Environmental Defense Fund — unsuccessfully. But my application to the Natural Resources Defense Council (NRDC) resulted in an interview. I felt elated when I saw they employed lawyers and scientists to bring citizen lawsuits on behalf of the environment, and they had projects from the Pacific Northwest with initiatives to protect salmon, to a nuclear non-proliferation group in Washington, D.C. Heeding that simple suggestion to pivot ended up leading to a thirty-year career in environmental-related work.

The first time I walked into the NRDC's retrofitted office on 20th Street in Chelsea, I knew I would do any job just to work there. Natural light came in from the vaulted ceiling and spilled down the open staircase. The leafy plants in the hallways gently swayed as the air recirculated frequently. There was no weird, unnatural, chemical office smell.

They hired me to work in the Coastal Program as a program assistant, which was secretarial, but the hours were good, and the people were smart, kind, and passionate about environmental protection. Though daily tasks included fetching Earl Grey tea and typing up the handwritten notes from my primary supervisor, I was honored to work directly with one of the original authors of the Clean Water Act.

Once our two-year leases were up, J.C. moved in with high school friends from when he lived in Japan. Their narrow loft apartment in Tribeca was in an artsy neighborhood, and his roommates' careers in film and acting meant their parties were fun. One of my roommates, Hillary, and I moved into the East Village on 7th Street between 1st and 2nd Avenues. We were in a tiny first-floor apartment with exposed brick and ventilation shafts between the buildings. I learned in graduate school that it was a "dumbbell" apartment, an 1880s design concept to improve air circulation between buildings, inadvertently resulting in residential dumping that led to the birth of public health regulations and the urban planning field.

Our apartment was a renovated one-bedroom, with a galley kitchen and storage space above the bathroom, accessible by a tiny, steep staircase suitable for goats. That storage space became my room when I put a futon and a reading lamp up there. We lived at the edge of dicey Alphabet City. Our neighbors were supermodels, musicians, and Ukrainians. One block south, 6th Street housed dozens of Indian restaurants emanating mouth-watering scents of curry. At Justine's tiny apartment in Greenwich Village, we ate dinner on top of her old suitcase, and she lit candles perched on a Chianti wine bottle covered in colored wax. The bathtub served double duty as the kitchen sink. As for me and J.C., the distance between Tribeca and the East Village made our hearts grow fonder, and we returned to dating and discovering the city, rather than doing laundry together. On weekends, we went out to hear live music at '90s institutions like the musty-smelling Knitting Factory and the Wetlands; we even heard Uncle Tupelo (later to become Wilco and Sun Volt), Juliana Hatfield, and the Lemonheads at the famous smoky rock club CBGB. My years of piano lessons gave me a trained ear and an appetite for live music. I got my exercise by taking African dance lessons, which was a welcome contrast to drill team.

During my second year at NRDC, I volunteered to help write a report on coastal beach closures called *Testing the Waters*. I stayed late to conduct research, tabulate data, and format the report, one of an annual series published by the Coastal Program. NRDC reports were released at press events that media covered in person. The work and my part on the production team energized me, and I believed the report could lead to coastal, county-level initiatives to reduce pollution that ended up on US beaches. The work planted a seed in me, a belief in environmental regulatory protection, which grew into my career.

My relationship with Dad was challenging during my time in New York. Dad told me he couldn't visit unless I agreed to have lunch with his new wife. I complained to a friend that the requirement was horseshit, that he was my father first — why should I have to acknowledge her? My wise friend asked if I wanted to have any relationship with my dad. If so, she said I should make the concession of having lunch so he could visit me in New York.

When Dad did come to New York, he marveled at the multitude of mushrooms at Dean & DeLuca grocery store. We went to see *Miss Saigon* on

Showing Dad around NYC after we reconnected.

Broadway, and he had tears in his eyes before the first song was over. He stood motionless, in awe, taking in the massive Temple of Dendur in its vast echoing room at the Met.

There's a saying by columnist Mary Schmich: "Live in New York City once, but leave before it makes you hard." In addition to finding my way in work and relationships, in New York I learned to be a subway commuter, ignoring unpleasant odors and focusing on the tap dancer, the bucket drummer, the *SNL* cast member sightings, and the vast, people-moving power of transit. I fed my curiosity with pottery and newswriting classes and sought out free music and museum exhibits. When dog-sitting for a colleague, I discovered NPR by way of the alarm clock, creating a lifelong public-radio habit. I knew which streets were busy, well-lit, and safe for a single woman walking home at night.

Though I loved NRDC, after two years, I recognized I couldn't rise in the company without a graduate degree. Around the same time, J.C. realized he felt no passion working as a copper and precious metals trader at Mitsubishi. He started researching architecture schools and planning to move to California to establish residency for in-state tuition. At the time, I was not interested in getting engaged. My parents' divorce was too raw, so I told J.C. I didn't want to be a wife because that seemed like a bad job. But we decided we were ready to move in together if we could both get jobs in San Francisco.

My final weeks in New York made it easier to leave. It was steamy hot; no number of showers could cool you off in the summer of 1993. J.C. and his brother were traveling overseas, so I escaped in my imagination by reading his letters. They were written on onionskin paper with red and blue striped edges, labeled PAR AVION, and smelled of Moroccan spices.

I sublet our apartment for a couple summer months to two film-school guys working on a movie set. When they told me they were living on the set, I agreed they could move in early, and we shared the apartment for two weeks. This was a benefit on the day our NRDC softball team played New York City's Planning Department. We were fielding, and my friend sprinted to make a heroic outfield catch that was coming to me — he didn't trust me to make the catch. I ducked, and he tried to jump over me but instead kicked me in the head going full speed. I saw stars and doubles of my hands in front of my face. My teammates took me home. I made the filmmaker roommates wake me up every hour that night to make sure my brain wasn't bleeding. So long, New York.

City by the Bay

San Francisco, 1993 – 1994

I secured another program assistant job with the NRDC in San Francisco working for the Forestry Program and started in late summer 1993. As in New York, the NRDC San Francisco office staff was a great group of people. I needed housing for a couple weeks before J.C. arrived, and my new colleagues set me up with two cat- and house-sitting gigs in Oakland. I eagerly awaited J.C.'s arrival after his own solo cross-country road trip from D.C. With only pay phones to connect us, I worried about his safe arrival. I hoped we would reconnect quickly after his adventures in Europe. In a bout of immaturity, I shed tears when my new supervisor denied my early departure from work on the day he arrived (now I can't believe I asked). Yet another NRDC coworker connected me with her landlord, through whom we quickly secured a dreamy apartment.

Despite the official but half-hearted objection from our parents, J.C. and I moved in together that fall. Ours was a multi-story, orange-brick building on the corner of Fulton and Scott, also the corner of Alamo Square Park, which bordered the beautiful Victorian "painted lady" houses that stairstep down the street and adorn tourist postcards of San Francisco. When we saw the spacious corner apartment on a high floor, the antique stove, wood floors, and large windows with a view of the Bay Bridge from one side of the apartment and the Golden Gate Bridge from the other, J.C. and I signed the lease.

Since Mom had much of her furniture in storage in Dallas, she generously sent an American Red Ball moving truck to help set us up. To our surprise, the movers kept bringing more and more furniture up the stairs to our apartment — a four-poster bed, a three-mirrored marble vanity, a love seat with Washington crossing the Delaware in the green and white fabric pattern, a whole wicker seating set, a heavy wooden glass-topped desk, a brass lamp, various decorative antiques, including a butter churn, a brass bed warmer, and an upright piano. We tossed some of Grandma Schmeil's handmade throw blankets over the couches and settled in. It looked cozy and familiar but spoke more about our childhood homes

With Sloan on our drive from Dallas to San Francisco, 1993.

than our new life together. When we hosted our holiday party (the first of dozens), one close friend we knew in New York said, "You all went from twenty to forty years old overnight!"

To prepare for architecture school applications, J.C. created a portfolio involving a range of projects from paintings to small sculptures to drawings in different media. He and I both took the GRE test; we reviewed our fat study volumes during the bus commute to our downtown offices. He worked at Charles Schwab, and the NRDC office was in SoMa (South of Market Street). I typed up legal documents and amicus curiae papers for the researchers and lawyers in the Forestry Program. They worked to protect endangered forest mammals such as the American Marten and Pacific Fisher, whose shared habitat was threatened by logging, urban development, and forest fires. My supervisors submitted public comments on environmental assessments, which foretold my career.

On weekends, J.C. and I explored the Headlands' cliffs and Muir Woods, north of the Golden Gate Bridge. The cold and wild Northern California coast provided a stark contrast to urban New York City. Visiting Stinson Beach or Mill Valley less than an hour from our apartment was a wonderful break from work. I took Brazilian and hip-hop dance lessons and was thrilled to perform for friends and family.

J.C. applied to architecture master's programs on the West Coast and in Texas. His interest in UT Austin, where some high-school classmates attended and where my parents went to university, surprised me. Having escaped Dallas, I had not seriously considered moving back to Texas, but I did hear good things about Austin. Friends who went to graduate school in the University of California system said, "Oh, you'll be able to find housing! The library will be open!" Sadly, at that time, the libraries were on a shortened schedule due to funding shortages in the UC system. We visited a friend who attended UCLA architecture school. His apartment was literally missing part of the roof, and on late nights, he slept on the roof of the architecture building. My ears perked up when I learned that UT Austin not only had resources, but also had an oil well on campus, which indicated to me that the school would stay open (now I know it's a historical artifact).

J.C. received several acceptances on the West Coast. I had resigned myself to applying to law school. During a vulnerable moment at NRDC, I was photocopying my application to take an LSAT prep course. As I complained, a colleague said, "Give me a break. My friend just started medical school at fifty years old. You have many paths available." I asked her what she studied in graduate school. "Planning." When I learned that she was referring to environmental planning, optimism filled me. There might have been a graduate school path for me yet.

To my surprise, of the schools where J.C. had been accepted, the program that interested me most was the Community and Regional Planning Program at UT Austin. It heavily focused on local environmental considerations. Reading about the program sparked my curiosity: Why is everyone talking about Barton Springs salamanders? What is the Edwards Aquifer? I summoned the courage to call the Planning Program office and ask if they had any spots available for the next year. I said my boyfriend was admitted to the architecture program and was considering it. To their credit, they scheduled phone interviews with the program director and a professor. They gave me two weeks to apply by snail mail. I scrambled to pull everything together. Within a month, I was offered a spot in the master's program.

In spring 1994, J.C. and I planned a getaway to Hopland, California, with the intention of decompressing after graduate school applications and deciding on next steps. We were both admitted to UT Austin, so our choice was clear. We could relax. We lounged in the bed and breakfast's hot tub, hiked, and drank locally brewed Red Tail Ale. When we stumbled upon an antique shop where a jeweler had retired and handed over his collection, I cautiously looked in the glass case. I tried on a modest white gold ring from the 1940s with a tiny diamond. We left without it, or so I thought.

J.C. and I flew down to Austin to see the school and meet with the professors before committing. I could see Austin was a unique part of Texas: I loved Town Lake, Barton Springs, and the laid-back vibe of the city. The architecture and planning schools sat across the street from each other, in different but equally beautiful buildings. The visit convinced us. We were warmly welcomed to a fresh chapter in Texas. Go Longhorns!

We also traveled to Dallas on that trip to visit Mom, who was dating a geologist-turned-Episcopal-priest named Bill Dockery. His two grown children had attended my high school. They were surprised their dad was dating his decorator, while my sister and I were surprised our mom was dating a priest. They got married that year, and Mom moved into his house on Colgate Avenue. After being on Mockingbird Lane for twenty years, then moving three times since then, we all felt grateful for her new little house with the wood-burning fireplace and a big magnolia tree. We had many lovely, combined family celebrations in that house; though it's odd to think of them as my stepbrother and stepsister since we were all adults when our parents married, we have thoroughly enjoyed spending time with the Dockery and Blair families.

By June, J.C. and I finalized plans to move to Austin for graduate school in August. That summer, the soccer World Cup was being held in the US, and Stanford hosted one game — J.C. went with several fraternity brothers. I didn't expect to see him until late, but he called me at the office to ask what time I would be home. I told him 6:30 or so. I became suspicious — what was he doing home early from a World Cup game? After work, I got off the bus and crossed Alamo Square Park as usual. When I entered our apartment, full of natural light before sunset, I smelled that J.C. had dinner on the stove and saw a nice bottle of wine on the set table.

He asked me to sit down and handed me a flat, rectangular box. It contained a dark blue linen-bound book entitled *Poems for a Princess* by J.C. Schmeil. My eyes filled with tears as I read poem after poem, with illustrations — some his own — on many pages. (In 1994, it was a feat to produce a real printed book of original work.) I laughed, and I cried, rereading serious and silly poems he wrote during our four-and-a-half year dating period. In that lovely apartment, presented with a beautiful meal, reading poems J.C. had written, recalling our time in San Francisco, New York, and Stanford, I was grateful for his patience, and I knew that he was the man for me. According to J.C., it took ages for me to read every word of every poem until I got to the last page that read, "Ashley, will you marry me?" He got down on one knee and presented me with a beautiful ring — the antique engagement ring from Hopland, plus blue sapphires on either side. I said yes and wrapped my arms around him, thrilled to be engaged and starting our next life chapter in Austin.

When packing up the San Francisco apartment, J.C. and I felt claustrophobic among the antiques and throw blankets. J.C. was about to embark on his architecture career, and his favorite styles were Japanese (Tadao Ando) and mid-century modern. It dawned on us that Mom would not have sent her most prized possessions to San Francisco, so we downsized by hosting a yard sale. We sold a few large pieces to friends. We then took picnic blankets to Alamo Square Park and laid out the things we wanted to sell to clear the way for defining our own style: the brass lamp, butter churn, and bed warmer (genuine American antiques). We parted ways with books, magazines, and miscellaneous items that, as a seller, you always think are going to be hot items, but nobody wants. When a man approached us with a grocery cart and offered to take away everything else for $25, we agreed.

My favorite sale that day was my Friday uniform from my high school Highland Belles drill team. The word "Captain" was embroidered in white script on the top left-hand side of the navy blue sleeveless top with a white and gold striped collar. This shirt went with a cheerleader-style pleated skirt. I couldn't imagine where I would ever wear it again, so I laid it on the blanket. When an attractive, muscular, tattooed girl (remember, this was 1994) in laced-up Doc Martens approached eyeing the uniform, I immediately told her she had to take it. I charged her no more than a few dollars. Having been away from preppy Highland Park for eight years, I felt satisfied with the radical act of conveying that uniform to a rock-and-roll girl.

Living in San Francisco, I loved the beauty of the city and the bay, the nearby redwoods, the smell of eucalyptus trees, Mission-style burritos, and City Lights Bookshop. In the one year I spent there, I enjoyed work, made friends, was admitted to graduate school, became engaged, and developed my own style. I wore cat-eyed reading glasses, black shoes with grommets I'd bought with friends, flowy pants, and vintage jewelry. I also found a new purpose — becoming a professional planner.

Part III: What We Choose

In our young independence, we moved from seeking our place beyond the homes where we grew up to choosing specific people and places that would constitute the homes of our adult lives. Choosing graduate school, cautiously returning to Texas, selecting a career in planning, then committing to marriage were life-defining events. Parenthood equaled holding up a mirror to my physical identity.

This phase of choosing also coincided with unforeseen opportunity. Our honeymoon destination became the subject of my graduate thesis, and travel to places that are now much restricted left us wide-eyed with wonder. Dancing at a harvest festival in the Four Girls Mountains of China sparked my contemplation of environmental justice.

When we seek out the world, we undock and sail into the horizon. Our choices set the tack before we drop anchor.

J.C.'s parents, Jerry and Vicki Schmeil, with us at our engagement party at my mom Sue and Bill's house in Dallas.

Hell Froze Over, and I Moved Back to Texas

Austin, Texas, and Belize, 1994 – 1996

I used to tell my parents I would not move back to Texas unless hell froze over, largely due to the forces that influenced my departure. I joke that it must have, because I did. In late summer 1994, J.C. and I drove from San Francisco to Austin in the black, two-door Honda Accord my dad got for me at (another) auction. When we crossed the Texas state line, a huge thunderstorm hit: loud, dramatic, rain pounding down in sheets or blowing horizontally across the windshield, no match for wiper blades. We saw lightning strike and scramble on the roadway just in front of us. We made our way slowly across miles of flat stretches of land, watching the light show in the black clouds, stopping briefly for cover under highway overpasses or at crowded gas stations until the storm cell passed. I hated driving through bad weather, but when safe inside, I loved a good Texas thunderstorm. I wanted J.C. to be impressed with the magnitude of the light show.

We rented an apartment in Hyde Park at Duval and 43rd Streets, and it reminded us of *Melrose Place*, with two floors of apartments, exterior walkways, and an internal landscaped courtyard. When the moving truck arrived from San Francisco, J.C. had to help a strong woman and a skinny man squeeze the piano around corners and into the apartment. We decorated the carpeted one-bedroom with the furniture we'd kept and added a few prints on the wall, including old sheet music and a New Mexico-style string of dried peppers in the kitchen.

We liked the neighborhood with its laundromat, Fresh Plus grocery store, Hyde Park bakery, and nearby gas station. After having lived in New York and San Francisco, we wondered why the neighborhood was so quiet at night. We took walks and listened to the sounds of chirping cicadas. One week, there were mating toads (alive and squooshed) all over the roads, having come up to street level from Waller Creek, which ran through Shipe Park. It looked like a plague, but we realized we could still experience nature within the city. Eventually we found the local restaurant and music scene — we just needed to drive to South Congress, Barton Springs Road, Sixth Street (before it was grungy), or South Lamar.

J.C. and I were both excited to start graduate school. He was pursuing a Master of Architecture degree in a four-year program, and I was pursuing a two-year Master of Science in Community and Regional Planning (the CRP program). We shared one car but could ride our cruiser bikes to classes in Goldsmith Hall for J.C. or Sutton Hall for me, across the campus roadway from each other.

The first day of classes, my professor Kent Butler said that in undergraduate school, the professors hold up the hoops and say, "Jump through the hoop!" In graduate school, the professors say, "The hoops are over there," meaning you have to choose the challenge you want to tackle, and you have to select the professors you want to hold the hoops for you — and how high. Having worked for other people the prior four years, I was excited to carve my own path. I worked hard in my classes. I studied at Flawn Academic Center, Perry-Castañeda Library (still with a card catalog), the student union, and the dusty stacks of the planning library in Sutton Hall.

For Urban Design, students were assigned to one of two studio options in Sutton Hall: a large, open studio with windows on the first floor, or "the tower," a small overflow studio on the top floor with a few desks and minimal light. Most students assigned to the tower did not work there, so I was often alone, highlighting layers of a topographic map (ridgelines, waterways, vegetation, development) with colored pencils on vellum. It didn't occur to me to ask to be moved to the other studio, or to just move my work downstairs for the bustling social experience. Many CRP students had jobs while in graduate school and left campus right after class, so it was difficult to find my bearings.

I was surprised to find myself feeling lonely in grad school. But life was quite different for J.C. He was in studio or class at Goldsmith most of the time. His first experience was to claim a desk in a design studio, since most drawing was done by hand until they learned computer-aided design toward the end of the program. Many students were young and straight out of undergraduate school. His studio experience was invigorating and competitive.

To make connections, I volunteered to be social chair for the CRP Student Organization and posted happy hour flyers in the architecture and planning buildings. J.C. and I joked that we were the link between planners (who thought architects were ivory tower types) and architects (who thought planners were paper pushers). Gradually, I got to know more students in the CRP program.

Since J.C. and I had a holiday party in San Francisco, we decided to have one in Austin. We invited friends from planning and architecture. I was embarrassed and disappointed when J.C. arrived at the party at the very end — still caught up with finishing an end-of-semester project. Unlike the papers planning students had to submit for finals, J.C. had large architecture projects that required inspiration from the muse, as well as tedious execution.

Another source of tension in our new life was that J.C. and I had known our friends in New York and San Francisco before we were engaged. Once we arrived in Austin, we felt labeled as the "engaged couple," which felt like a scarlet letter on us — we assumed people were thinking, "They won't be any fun, they're practically married." We were planning our Austin wedding for the following June using the single, skinny book available about options for marrying in the city.

My stress piqued when I thought J.C. had a crush on a valley girl from the architecture program (turns out that all his friends did, too). I was tired of being alone in our tiny apartment at night, wondering where he was. We had no cell phones and didn't use email for personal reasons yet. With my parents' divorce subconsciously fueling fears of infidelity, we had one stupid argument at a Michaels craft store. I challenged him about where his attention was going. I said if he wasn't interested in me, I had my eye on someone else. He promptly said, "Oh, that good looking guy who told you he was planning to join the Navy or open a smoothie shop?" (He nailed it, of course. I really didn't like the guy but wanted confirmation of J.C.'s interest.) Fortunately, he reassured me and drew me a bubble bath complete with candles and a glass of wine.

Soon thereafter, J.C. moved us out of our tiny apartment into a duplex for rent on Maplewood Avenue. We loved the neighborhood, with two-story, concrete masonry units, cinder block construction, and covered with stucco and paint typical of the Delwood historic district. The neighborhood, east of I-35 and north of 38th ½ street, had well-established trees, friendly front porches and balconies, and was anchored by Maplewood Elementary School. We moved in between semesters. It was the fresh start we needed. We had an upstairs unit with wood floors and views of trees, cicadas, June bugs, and fireflies at night.

Now confident we were moving forward with our wedding plans, I concluded I needed to work part-time to stay busy and make some money. When I applied for a job as the volunteer coordinator for the Lower Colorado River Authority (LCRA), I told the interviewer I could do a full-time job in half the time and was hired. For two years, I supported volunteer water-quality monitors throughout the Lower Colorado River Basin as part of the Colorado River Watch Network. The job involved meeting with volunteers wherever they lived (from Brownwood to Wharton), resupplying their water testing chemicals, and collecting data sheets. I worked with all ages of volunteers and prized having a job that took me outside into nature. I believed in protecting our waterways and the mission of helping people steward the environment in their own backyards. Working at LCRA was a great counterbalance to my graduate school studies and made it easier to handle J.C.'s long hours in the design studio. I felt anchored, useful, and responsible working and earning some income.

On Marriage

Austin and Belize, 1995 – 1996

In June we turned our attention to getting excited about the wedding. In the apartment a day or so before the festivities, we hosted friends, some of whom tried to sleep on the balcony but moved inside because the summer insects were too loud. We loved sharing our new hometown. Family and friends from all over the country came to attend the wedding. Our rehearsal dinner was at Granite Cafe on 29th Street and Shoal Creek, where embarrassing toasts were made, but cut off early since J.C. was hungover and needed to be sick in the restroom. The day of the wedding, my fractured family visited at our Austin home on Maplewood Avenue, and I've never been so grateful for the Dallas Cowboys, the one subject my grandmother Gigi, my mother, and Dad's wife could discuss innocuously. Since Mom remarried, too, both parental parties stuck with their own guests, and thankfully, no issues arose.

We held both wedding and reception outside on the grounds of The French Legation, the former home of the French chargés d'affaires when Texas was a Republic. It overlooked downtown from a hill on East 7th Street. Aunt Becky helped coordinate and fussed over the details. J.C. had invited eight Sigma Chi friends to be groomsmen, so I invited an equal number of bridesmaids — my sister, cousins, childhood friends, and college friends. J.C. designed the wedding program cover replicated on handheld fans. We had hurricane lamps over candles lining the aisle — a couple of them burst, adding excitement to the service. Bill, mom's second husband, married us under the weeping crepe myrtle trees. Dad walked me down the aisle (how strange to think of the phrase "gave me away"). We wrote our own heartfelt vows and friends read "It Was a Quiet Way (#1053)" by Emily Dickinson and "On Marriage" by Kahlil Gibran.

After the service, the caterers converted the ceremony area into a dance floor. We served a partially seated dinner, meaning we had tables around the grounds where guests could eat after visiting the local Mexican food buffet. We enjoyed Celis White beer and Bonny Doon rosé wine. The live oaks provided a beautiful canopy for the casual reception and dancing to live music from the local band Cenzontle, who serenaded us from the elevated porch of the historic home. Many attendees came heavily sunburned from spending time at Hippy Hollow, the nude beach at Lake Travis.

J.C. and I danced and laughed to "Crazy" by Patsy Cline, sung with a slightly Spanish-tinged accent. Dancing made guests feel even hotter, so the groomsmen proceeded to remove their tux shirts and wear just their off-white vests and bow ties. After cake and toasts, our guests showered birdseed over J.C. and me and sent us off to spend the night at a Hyde Park bed and breakfast. We collapsed with exhaustion after eating the plate of food kindly dropped off by family friends. J.C. and I left the next day for a week in beautiful Belize, where we explored the jungle in the Mountain Pine Ridge area and the beaches of Ambergris Caye. We swam in waterfall-fed pools, watched Blue Morpho butterflies flap their iridescent wings, learned about medicinal properties of the rainforest, and snorkeled with rays and nurse sharks. We spent a day on a catamaran, and I remembered sailing days when nature first instilled a sense of wonder in me.

Irreverent again, I chose to keep my last name. Mom was shocked, but I told her I had just started to claim my identify and my signature as L. Ashley McLain. (My sister and I were the last of our line of McLains, so both my sons have McLain as a second middle name.)

Our second year of graduate school was busy. We continued with our coursework, and I kept working part-time at LCRA, plus I was editor of the Colorado River Watch Network newsletter, *Aqua Vitae*. I took on additional activities, since studio time continued to be all-consuming for J.C. I joined the editorial staff of *Planning Forum*, a new journal, and became the editor of *Nexus*, the newsletter for the planning program. My favorite feature article I wrote was called "Austin on 47 Cents a Day," based on my interview with Professor Peter Coltman. He was one of the first CRP students at UT, having moved to Austin from South Africa around 1960. When he arrived, it took days for the administration to locate his scholarship, so he navigated the quaint-at-the-time city with almost no money. A fantastic professor, he taught me to respectfully consider local input for planning projects that affect communities.

To complete the CRP degree, students had to write a professional report (PR) that aligned with an internship or a thesis. Most students prepared a PR, but I had the time to write a thesis since J.C. had at least another year in graduate

Top: Walking down the aisle at Austin's French Legation after exchanging vows on June 24, 1995 — a very hot day. Bottom: Honeymoon in Belize.

school. I selected my thesis advisors: Dr. Mugerauer, who taught History, Theory, and Ethics of Planning, and Dr. Manners from the geography program.

I found a topic involving a project in Belize, which gave me the chance to go back there. A gorgeous country, full of natural and archaeological resources; it wasn't touristy at the time. I wrote a travel grant application and received a substantial award to spend a month in Gales Point, Belize, and two weeks in Wisconsin. The connection between the two was Dr. Horwich, a researcher from Wisconsin who worked to help create the community baboon sanctuary in Belize. I compared the concept of community-based conservation in both locations.

My plan was to distribute, collect, and analyze survey questionnaires about the basic concepts of community-based conservation and obstacles to its implementation. I quickly learned I had to complete the forms myself based on verbal interviews, due to the low literacy rate. I spoke at the community center about my project and tried to get as many surveys completed as possible. The richness of the experience came from spending time with the local people and hearing their stories. I learned the concepts of ecotourism and community-based conservation are difficult to advocate for where the birds, mammals, sea turtles, and plants that are rare in the world are locally plentiful. I took my nineteen-year-old sister with me as my photographer and companion. She snapped amazing photos of nature, people, and culture — we still have the slides in an old carousel high in a closet.

For accommodations, we rented rooms from women who were part of a women-run co-op and ate meals at other homes to spread around our economic impact. (In retrospect, I'm proud we supported the co-op.) There was one luxury hotel at the end of the isthmus where many residents worked. We never went there because we felt close to the locals, and the hotel felt inappropriate and anachronistic. We hired men — Moses and his sons Boombay and Popsey — to guide us into the bush to look for tapirs and jabiru storks, and for boat rides in the lagoon to see manatees. We drank Guinness at Gentle's Cool Spot, and I used the payphone there to call J.C. once a week where he was working in Seattle for his architect uncle. I learned that Mr. Gentle didn't care for the youth mission groups that came to Gales Point because they didn't buy beer, and they camped on properties owned by non-locals, putting very few of their first-world dollars into the local economy.

My sister came with me to Wisconsin as well, where we lived in a motel for two weeks. We canoed down the crookedest river in the state, the Kickapoo River. It was not affected by the Ice Age, apparently, so it not only has an interesting configuration, but its watershed is also home to many endangered plant, bird, and amphibian species. I conducted interviews with many people who wanted to create an ecotourism destination and butted heads with developers who previously attempted to impound the river for traditional tourism purposes by creating lake-front property. The development/conservation debate was easier to document in Wisconsin compared to Belize due to the political and legal systems in the US. Institutional systems and safeguards provided a framework within which to

Dressed up for dinner for my December graduation from University of Texas master's program in Community and Regional Planning.

function in Wisconsin, whereas those systems in Belize were less developed and less reliable.

Since I was writing a thesis, I enrolled in UT for a fifth semester. Fall semester, J.C. had been selected for a stage, or internship, in Paris. He would be working with Christian de Portzamparc, a Pritzker Prize-winning architect. I continued to work at LCRA and took independent study credits to finish my degree, along with conversational French. I was determined to submit my thesis, finish work at LCRA, and sell my car to move to Paris with him by the end of 1996.

A few days after the deadline, I submitted my thesis. I was late because it had to be printed in a particular way and perfect bound, and we also had to submit a copy on a CD. Nothing was turned in electronically in those days. Though I technically graduated in spring 1997, I participated in the December graduation, which included a nice dinner held in Goldsmith Hall. The graduating group was small, so the program director shared a bit about each graduate. When they read out the long list of my activities, I explained that I had to stay busy because I was married to an architecture student. I was proud to receive the award for Outstanding Graduate Thesis. Despite my initial insecurity at UT, during my time there, I grew not only in my relationship, but also academically, intellectually, and professionally.

Exhausted from moving out of our apartment and preparing for half a year overseas, J.C. and I packed up our REI frame backpacks and carry-ons with as much as we could fit, caught a flight to Charles de Gaulle airport, and arrived in Paris on New Year's Eve.

The City of Light

Paris and Russia, 1997

The Seine was frozen. Chunks of ice bobbed in the river, and the city fountains were frozen solid. Our roommate shared a hotel room with us for a few days until we found an apartment. We scoured through ads in the newspaper and made calls, shivering in a phone booth. J.C. studied in the French city of Tours in college, so he was our spokesperson. Fortunately, we found an apartment on Avenue de l'Observatoire near the Luxembourg Gardens in St. Germain and the Port-Royale RER rail stop in the 5th arrondissement. It was a walk-up with a dark wooden spiral staircase. There were two bedrooms, a tiny kitchen, a common room, and a bathroom off the entry hall.

I preferred to be busy, and J.C. was an artist; I would have dutifully tromped off to my internship, and he would have happily sketched at a café along the river. But our roles were reversed. He enthusiastically headed to work at Portzamparc's office, and I ventured out into the city. We had tiny budgets: J.C.'s internship was part of tuition (a work-study arrangement). All the money I had came from selling the Honda. To try to make our francs go further, I quickly learned that it was cheaper to get a croissant and a café au lait standing at a copper bar counter versus sitting at a café table, so I spent my mornings squeezed up to such counters, scanning through my Paris guidebook and trying to figure out how to get a job.

I had bad jet lag, so after the guys went to work, I filled the bathtub and soaked up the warmth, listening to French conversation cassette tapes to revive the French I'd learned in high school. Once the electric bill arrived at the end of the month, we were shocked to learn that our bill — my baths —cost us about $600. There went my budget!

I visited several art museums but soon became bored of being on my own. I felt depressed because I was having a difficult time talking to people. I didn't have a job or set schedule, nights were long, days were short, and J.C. was having a great time. Our roommate spent time mostly with his coworkers. I began to realize I needed to be working and busy to be happy.

Outside our home in Paris at 30 Avenue de l'Observatoire.

I found a listing for teaching English in the suburb of Saint-Cloud at the American School of Paris. I was hired to teach French students English when the American students were on spring break. I also found the United Nations Environment Programme (UNEP). Their Industry and Environment Division had a tourism department, and I contacted them to ask about volunteer opportunities. One supervisor was impressed with my master's thesis on ecotourism and offered to let me work (unpaid) a few days a week.

At the school in Saint-Cloud, I was assigned middle-school students. Having never taught English to French middle schoolers, I combed through the bookstores in the St. Germain district on Paris' Rive Gauche, where I found many workbooks that taught British English. Armed with my workbooks, I enthusiastically commuted on the train, transferred to a bus, picked up a jambon fromage sandwich on pain Poilâne at the bus stop, and walked the last few minutes to the school. The students loved having an American teacher and helped me with my French. As a treat, we would play American songs on the cassette player, and of course they knew all the words: No Doubt's "Just a Girl" was their favorite. The school supervisor liked my teaching style, apparently, because the parents loved that their kids had spring break homework.

I was asked to return for a couple weeks in the summer to teach English again, as well as computer science — in French — and I did. My grasp of computers was limited, but it didn't matter in 1997 because computers were peripheral to life, rather than central, as they are today. The paychecks I earned boosted our ability to enjoy the city's bars and restaurants.

My French improved greatly once I signed up for lessons at Langue Onze language school in the 11th arrondissement. In Intermediate French, my teachers spoke and moved through material quickly. We had homework assignments on worksheets that we carried around with our pocket-sized French-English dictionaries. The best thing about the lessons were the (other) students from other countries, often Germany. The teachers regularly invited us out for drinks and discussion after class.

J.C. and I walked everywhere or took the Metro. We frequently visited the Luxembourg Gardens to walk along the trails. Witnessing sophisticated, urban life influenced us as people. We looked through the eyes of an architect and a planner — what constitutes beauty? What design inspires community? We admired the cafes with their front walls open for business — not small doors, but whole walls that were lifted to the ceiling to remove the separation between the inside bar and the café tables outside. We savored the smell of coffee roasting, buttery food simmering, carafes of house wine open on the tables, the sun shining through and coloring the white tablecloths with streaks of golden or claret. Everyday life was beautiful in Paris in springtime.

While in France, we got the news that J.C.'s grandmother had passed away and left him a little money. He decided she would want us to have an adventure. Our college friend had moved to Russia and married a local, so we flew to Moscow in June. They gave us a grand tour: Café Margarita, made famous by Bulgakov's *Master and Margarita*; the Kirov ballet dancing to Tchaikovsky; the gorgeous and deeply buried Metro system (which doubles as a bomb shelter) built in the 1930s to celebrate communism. The year 1997 marked the 850th anniversary of the city of Moscow, so the ornate orthodox buildings in Red Square were gleaming for the celebrations.

Moscow was full of paradoxes. Many people were poor, but the ruble was strong. One night, we ate at a Cuban restaurant — many Cuban students studied in Moscow. For two burritos, two margaritas, chips and salsa, J.C. and I paid the equivalent of $147 (almost $300 today). International fashion stores were opening alongside the older, modest local bread and donut shops. Women stood outside the donut shops' doors holding hooks with single items of clothing hanging on

Outside the Hermitage during our Russia trip from Paris.

them to sell, one in each hand. I stood in a Russian Orthodox church listening to a cappella singing in the vaulted chapel shaped like a plus sign from a bird's-eye view, surrounded by the staring eyes of Mother Mary. In the dank bathroom nearby, I felt the cold of the clay floor and smelled the stench of urine from the wire waste basket full of notes, letters, and newspaper that people used in lieu of toilet tissue.

We took an overnight train to St. Petersburg to visit the Hermitage Museum, filled with ornate paintings, and Catherine the Great's summer palace. In the square, we bought bread from simply dressed women in a modest shop. During the summer White Nights, the sun hardly set. From a vendor, we purchased Russian nesting dolls painted like politicians from the past millennium, ending with Gorbachev. (Yeltsin served as President of Russia when we visited.)

Our friend invited us to stay at the dacha (country cottage) he and his father-in-law built. They grew cucumbers, tomatoes, and fresh dill. The sauna roof was a planted garden. The berries we picked in the woods, the unpasteurized pivo (beer) served from plastic liter bottles, and the caviar and grilled salmon we ate were unforgettable. I didn't expect Russian food to be so outstanding, but our hosts had high standards and were very proud.

Back in Paris, one day we explored La Petite Ceinture — the Little Belt railroad from the 1850s that encircles the city. Much of it is abandoned. Friends from French class invited us to meet them at La Flèche d'Or, a railroad maintenance building turned nightclub. It was near Père Lachaise Cemetery where Chopin, Jimi Hendrix, and many other famous people were buried. We hopped over a chain-link fence and started walking along the railroad tracks. We passed all types of

Living and working in Paris during J.C.'s architecture internship.

buildings, from homes to warehouses to empty lots. Our friends pointed out the most interesting areas: a loading dock for a slaughterhouse turned into a canvas for colorful graffiti, for example. Nature had reclaimed many buildings for itself. Our friends brought bread, cheese, and wine in their backpacks, which we shared under a shade tree. That day, I remember speaking as much as J.C. — his French was more precise, but I could communicate well by that time. We felt free, urban, worldly, happy, and ambitious — we always wanted to be able to travel (and knew we'd have to have the resources to do so).

When you know you're going home, your heart and mind become nostalgic. We recognized that although we loved Paris, we would always be outsiders there. We adored the gorgeous city but also felt surrounded by centuries of the looming past. We started to miss the newness of the US, the entrepreneurial spirit, the youthful energy, Tex-Mex food, and American music.

Dancing with local people in Sichuan Province.

Traveling on a Road While It's Being Built

Beijing and Sichuan Province, China, 1997

When I was working for the UNEP, I was shocked to receive an invitation to attend a mission trip representing the organization. There was to be a spring conference on ecotourism in and near the city of Chengdu in Sichuan, a province in Southwestern China. My supervisor selected me to attend because I wrote my graduate thesis on community-based conservation and prepared an educational handout about ecotourism for UNEP. UNEP planned and funded everything for me to travel alone to Chengdu by way of Beijing for about a week. I was expected to meet with the head of the Chinese equivalent of the EPA in Beijing, then fly to Chengdu and meet the conference organizers. I was in the right place at the right time; it resulted in an unforgettable cultural exchange, the likes of which few people ever get to experience.

I wasn't in the expatriate part of Beijing for the beginning of my trip: I stayed in a Chinese business hotel because a Chinese UNEP staff person had made the arrangements for me. I equipped myself with a travel bag, a copy of Paul Theroux's *Riding the Iron Rooster* about his travels riding the old steam trains across China, and a fat red-and-white copy of *Lonely Planet China*. The guide's small, boxed timeline contained a concise summary of Chinese history, in which the entire existence of the modern US fell within the scope of the last, most recent chronological entry. That humbled and intimidated me. I remembered visiting China through the People-to-People student ambassador program in 1986, when we could still see some people wearing all-blue outfits from the Mao regime. I thought about the Tiananmen Square Massacre that dominated my summer at Amnesty International in 1989 — of course I had questions about free speech and democracy. But this was 1997, and *Lonely Planet* indicated I was safe there as a single woman, because any violence against Americans, including women, was severely punished.

I wandered the streets for a couple days, taking the wrong bus and ending up next to a tree full of small cages with songbirds for sale. I saw women sweeping the dirty streets with straw brooms. I waited to cross the street at a traffic light next to a barber who had a chair, a cloth, and a pair of scissors, cutting hair right on the street corner. I visited the Temple of the Moon. I went out to dinner and laughed at the English translation of one of the dishes: Deep Fried Peasant.

In Beijing, I had one meeting with a representative from the Chinese agency for environmental protection. I took a cab from the hotel, but the driver got lost. We found ourselves in the middle of the hutongs, dense traditional dwellings first constructed in the Yuan dynasty in the thirteenth and fourteenth centuries. The streets were almost all too narrow to accommodate a taxi with the bustling street-level human activity, so I got out and walked toward the looming modern building that rose up into the air a block away. I mainly remember exchanging business cards and shaking hands, wondering what they thought of this twenty-nine-year-old "UNEP representative." Back at the hotel, there was always a steaming hot thermos of floral-scented jasmine tea on the bedside table, a lovely way to settle down for sleep.

I navigated the local airport to travel from Beijing to Chengdu. When I arrived, I settled into the hotel and went out for dinner alone. I found a restaurant that served the famous "Pock-Marked Grandma's Mapo Dofu," a spicy Sichuan tofu specialty. A moving river with fish in it was built into the restaurant floor. While I ate my delicious dinner, I read my books.

The next day, the conference hosts picked me up from the hotel. They were horrified that I had spent several days alone. From that point forward, I was always driven to my destinations and accompanied by a translator.

The conference started off with meetings, presentations, and social events. Attendees included the president of an adventure travel company in San Francisco, an architect helping prepare Australia's facilities for the upcoming 2000 Summer Olympics, scholars from all over China, and me — the unpaid UNEP intern. We sat on stage during an Earth Day celebration. The young adult students in attendance cheered for us. We visited the Wolong Giant Panda Reserve and got our photos taken petting an enormous panda, distracted with a stick of bamboo. The people I met were amazing hosts. My translator graciously asked: "Forgive me, but I don't understand America. I know you have nice streets. But what about education?

Surprising photo op at Wolong Giant Panda Nature Reserve.

Here in China, we may not have as many paved roads, but even smaller towns have public universities." I didn't, and don't, have a good answer for that prioritization.

The pinnacle of the event was a group trip to a site proposed as a community-based tourism destination called Four Girls Mountain. We set out in a few vans. A jolly spirit filled the air as some of the attendees — much to my surprise — sang songs and impersonated politicians in the news at the time. Everyone laughed full-belly laughs and kept spirits high for the long trip. As we ascended to high elevations, the air started to thin. As we drove into banks of clouds, our van stopped, baffling me. On hopped a smiling man in a lab coat carrying a tank of oxygen. He stopped at every passenger and allowed us each to inhale several gulps of oxygen from a mask he passed from person to person.

We continued along the narrow, unpaved road up the mountain side. The geology consisted of slate, a dark green-grey stone material that poked out of the rough-cut hillsides where it had been cut away. As we ascended higher, we saw workers using sharp instruments and baskets to cut the road into the hillside by hand. On top of a mountain. With no pavement, no asphalt, no railings, no gas stations, no restrooms. Perhaps they were dropped off in the morning and retrieved at the end of a long workday.

At one point, we stopped at a religious site close to the Tibetan Plateau. Tibetan prayer flags fluttered in the gentle breeze; the bamboo poles stuck into the ground among a grouping of teetering pillars of stones — cairns erected as memorials. The scenery took my breath away. And we could not see the road ahead at all.

Back in the van, we proceeded carefully along the "road." Our guide was on a walkie-talkie communicating with the other van drivers. We heard an incomprehensible exchange, and he indicated with his hands in front of him, palms facing down as if flattening a pillow. I understood this to mean "be calm." Suddenly, we heard and felt an explosion! I was sitting with an Australian, and we started taking photos of our loved ones out of our wallets to share. The blast frightened us all. A translator told us not to worry, they were blasting into the hillside. The road to our destination was not actually built yet, but they were trying hard to cut a path for us to drive through. After an eternity of nervous discomfort, they directed us to get out and walk. Our luggage would be brought along by a different route.

We walked along a narrow, slate half-road with no guardrail, clinging to the mountainside. We started to descend and saw in front of us an old logging camp and a coursing river. Once we made it to our destination and found our assigned rooms, we started to soak in the sheer beauty of the area. We were in the mountains at the edge of the timber line. We could see bare mountaintops all around. The river ran right under us (and the rustic bathroom a wooden structure with holes opening straight into the river). Despite the rudimentary sanitation, it remained the wildest, most beautiful river I have ever seen.

That evening, they treated us to a lavish welcome ceremony complete with locally made grain liquor and multi-course meals, including every variety of handmade noodle topped with fresh, mysterious sauces. The next day we rode on burros with wooden saddles up paths lined with blooming azalea trees to a celebration of the harvest with delectable grilled lamb. Young girls danced around us in their traditional clothing with modern tennis shoes. I felt like royalty that day. I felt humiliated when the village representatives, the elders, sincerely asked me if I could help them become designated as a World Heritage Site. I told them I would write a detailed report to convey their request to my supervisors at UNEP, but I had little influence and could make no promises.

The extreme emotions I felt that day ranged from fear for my life if our vehicle disappeared off the side of a mountain to wonder and profound gratitude for our hosts who shared pride in their region and their precious festival feast.

The locals were left picking up after the celebration, cleaning the rooms in the logging camp, and figuring out how to deal with our trash. I wondered, were they happy to share their bounty with us, or would some of them go without their traditional feasts? When our vans took off to return to Chengdu, rocking back

Four girls at Four Girls (Siguniang) Mountain in rural Sichuan Province.

and forth over the uneven slate road, I wondered if the locals' cultural tourism dream would be realized. On the sobering trip back to the city, we passed through industrial towns belching black coal smoke into the sky.

I cherish my photo of four serious girls in their decorated clothing, ribbons in their hair, rosy cheeks, and matching tennis shoes with the bare mountaintops in the background. These are my four girls of Four Girls Mountain. What would their future hold? What could I do to make a difference? Was ecotourism part of the answer? How could one protect the wild mountain rivers halfway around the world? Would anyone at the UNEP share my report, or would they file it on a shelf because relations with China were commonly tricky? The image of those girls foreshadowed my work at the intersection of people and the environment. In the natural environment, some species are more vulnerable than others, just as some people are more vulnerable than others in the human environment. I didn't know it yet, but I was about to embark on decades of work centered on the concept of environmental justice.

Finally celebrating J.C.'s graduation from UT with a Master of Architecture degree.

The Grind

Austin, 1997 – 1998

After leaving Paris to return to the US, we visited J.C.'s parents. They had recently learned that Caterpillar (the agriculture and construction equipment company) was relocating J.C.'s father, Jerry, to Singapore. We helped with some packing at the house. J.C. unearthed his throwing stars and other weapons acquired from Japan to bring home to Austin. J.C.'s mother, Vicki, liked her life in Vienna but rallied for Singapore — as she had done many times before when, as a young mother, she moved her sons from Geneva to Stockholm to Ivory Coast to Tokyo. We made plans to visit them in Singapore at Christmas.

Before leaving Paris, I started looking for jobs. There were a handful of environmental companies in Austin at the time. Espey, Huston & Associates was the most well-known, but I had already received a rejection postcard from them. I found Hicks & Company, applied, and received an opportunity to interview. I interviewed with owners Tom and Sandra. Their story interested me: They met in the Peace Corps in Africa; he was an attorney, and she had studied water resources. I liked the idea of working for a woman-owned firm.

My first office was in the computer graveyard, in a far corner, with a desk from TOPS used office furniture. I was assigned to write a section of an Environmental Impact Statement (EIS) document about socioeconomic impacts along a proposed roadway in north central Austin. I rolled up my sleeves, tracked down a copy of a census map at Texas Natural Resource Conservation Commission (TNRCC — or "Trainwreck" as it was called until they changed their name to Texas Commission on Environmental Quality), found the CDs that contained census information, and started collecting and analyzing socioeconomic data. This felt high-tech to me because in graduate school, we had to go to the library and get census data from hard copy books. State Highway 45 was the first socioeconomic document section I wrote in what ended up being dozens upon dozens of similar project- and geography-specific environmental studies.

I liked working in an office with archeologists, architectural historians, biologists, botanists, geographic information systems (GIS) mappers, and planners. They were all wired differently, so it made for an interesting anthropological study. On Fifth and Powell Streets, the office was less than a mile from the rental J.C. and I had found. The tiny backhouse was on lovely Maufrais Street (a name also stamped in concrete sidewalks throughout Austin), dense with cottages in the historic central Austin neighborhood of Clarksville. We walked to the backhouse via the driveway and were pleased to see a pretty limestone block wall. The little house had an entry room, study, one bedroom, galley kitchen, miniscule bathroom, and wooden deck with an outside, overhead fan. The landlord was installing ferns and leafy, shade-tolerant plants around the house and under the cedar elm tree. There would be a lion-head water fountain near the front door. As soon as it was finished, we moved in.

Though I could have walked to work, I admit I drove to save time, and so I could pick up J.C. from grad school after work. He'd come home for dinner and return to the studio afterward until midnight. He had challenging classes and professors, plus he couldn't work from home. I joked that I was dating Jon Stewart of *The Daily Show*. More than once, I woke up with a start thinking J.C. had come home, only to realize I was looking at a coat on a hook.

There was one phone in the architecture studio. I liked J.C. to call our home phone and let me know his schedule (most of which was spent working into the night at the studio). Meanwhile, I kept busy with work and hung out with my coworkers. One worked at a restaurant called Shaggy's on South Congress, near a house shared by two other coworkers. At the time, South Congress was a sleepy hodge-podge of stores, including a tile store, a guns and ammo store, a by-the-hour motel, and a porn theater. But Shaggy's was a hip Caribbean-inspired restaurant with live music and good vibes that helped pioneer the redevelopment of South Congress Avenue.

That Christmas, as planned, J.C. and I flew halfway around the world to spend the holidays on the equator with my in-laws. J.C.'s parents lived high up in a residential tower that his mother beautifully decorated— she always settled in regardless of how long the family would be stationed in a particular location. She deserves credit for her sons enjoying their international upbringing. The family's international life always brought cultural richness and diversity to my relationship with J.C. We visited the distinct Singapore cultural centers — Chinese, Malay, and

Indian. We ate my father-in-law's favorite spicy, fresh chili crab at the hawker market stalls and tried exotic fruits, like the spiky, red, creamy, sweet rambutan.

J.C. received a travel grant to study Batak architecture in Indonesia, so we took a side trip to Sumatra. In Medan, we squeezed onto a local bus blasting Indonesian techno music and sat next to an old woman with bright red betel juice dripping out of the wrinkled corners of her mouth. We visited a traditional village where residents still lived in large, triangular, communal Batak houses with ornately carved thresholds and farm animals living underneath. J.C. snapped dozens of photos with his SLR camera. We took a ferry boat across volcanic Lake Toba to spend a couple days scootering past ancient banyan trees, topped with massive storks' nests on Samosir Island. We spent one night in a lovely hotel overlooking Lake Toba for the equivalent of $4. Heading back to Singapore, we took a huge old station wagon to the Medan airport. The driver was delighted to learn we were from Austin, and in broken English, he rattled off a list of favorite musicians, including Willie Nelson and Stevie Ray Vaughan. The people we met in Indonesia were friendly, and Texas music connected us as global neighbors from opposite sides of the planet.

Back in Austin, I continued to work hard on my projects at Hicks & Company to demonstrate my capabilities. I put in extra hours and became increasingly eager for J.C. to be done with the grind of graduate school. He told me our friend would be getting married in Bolivia in the spring, but it conflicted with his graduation from architecture school. Though we usually loved to travel, I told him no way were we going to South America. That specific UT Austin graduation ceremony was for us — for me, too — for surviving his schedule in "Architorture" school. I was done being an architecture widow.

Graduation time finally arrived. J.C.'s parents came to town, and we attended the ceremony at Goldsmith Hall. We went out to dinner, and J.C. almost collapsed into his plate of food, exhausted from the semester. When it was over, he slept for days. We had survived graduate school together, the first of many milestones we'd share as a team.

Desktop memories 2007–2021; the jar opener was my favorite bit of conference swag when we founded CMEC to help clients "get a grip on environmental regulations."

Go Where You're Appreciated

Austin, 2007 – 2017

"Work within your sphere of influence or go where you're appreciated." This advice has been a core principle for my professional decisions. At a leadership conference, I was a rising project manager among senior staff, mostly men, who were taking this same four-weekend leadership training.

What I realized during the training was that, after close to ten years at my first consulting company, I had some frustrations with the leadership. I had tried unsuccessfully to broach the topics with the company owners (particularly succession planning). At the conference, I publicly asked the question: What if I have some differences with the leadership of the company? What should I do? The answer was, "Work within your sphere of influence or go where you're appreciated." Ultimately, for me that meant leaving the company and cofounding my own. Going where I was appreciated meant taking the leap to try being the boss — and to learn the lessons that would come from that experience, good or bad.

I have shared that lesson many times with many people, even employees. If they felt they could not grow in a certain area, then they should consider a different technical specialty, geography, professional goal, or different company altogether. The larger the company, the more important it was to define your sphere of influence.

The first time I really had to keep a serious secret (besides the early weeks of pregnancy) was when I decided to start a company. My coworker Larry at the consulting company asked me to lunch one day and asked if I was interested in starting a company. We would be partners along with his wife Lorie to get the woman-owned business certification. I knew her socially, but he assured me she could help with operations, since she had her master's degree in information science. The idea had never occurred to me, but I respected his business savvy and intelligence, and I was honored that he respected my work ethic and capabilities. I shared his concern that we shouldered many projects and client relations but were not part of personnel or company financial decisions, despite having the title of

Principal at our current company. But starting a new company from scratch was a risky move. I decided to sleep on it.

When I consulted J.C. about the prospect, he encouraged me. After all, he had gone out on his own, and his work was going well. We had some money in the bank, and he was willing to be the breadwinner while we launched. I realized my father, my mother, my aunt, and Uncle Archie all worked for themselves in some capacity. I decided to pursue it. Why not? Irreverently, I left the company where I had a leadership role and relative comfort to cofound my own company.

I bought a yellow and black book on starting a business from the *For Dummies* series that was popular in the 1990s and 2000s. We decided to call ourselves Cox|McLain Environmental Consulting, Inc., Cox being first since there were two Coxes and one McLain. We created a new company founded by one ecologist and one planner, with Lorie holding down the fort administratively until she could join us full-time, once their youngest son started kindergarten. We would provide the same services we had provided at our former employer, that being National Environmental Policy Act compliance for infrastructure projects, but with Larry and me at the helm. My partners and I wrote a business plan together and decided we would give notice at our then firm in August 2007. J.C. created a logo and website for us based on a photo of an agave plant leaf in our front yard, spun around into a green starburst shape.

That whole year working on the business plan, I was gaining courage and agency, excited to found a company. I was intent on creating policies and protocols (developing a printed employee manual, establishing a family leave policy, etc.). I was excited to try my hand in a leadership role without someone above me. I also concluded that if we failed, people would still respect us for trying.

By that point, our sons were in early elementary school, and J.C. and I decided we could live frugally (other than the cost of daycare). Starting the business didn't require a huge investment — just office space and computer equipment. We could handle living on J.C.'s salary for a few months. He and I joked that the boys would be fine living on a diet of ramen, as long as we added edamame or eggs for protein. It felt good to be scrappy, to make sacrifices in pursuit of a better future. J.C. was a devoted father and thankfully had flexibility in his architecture schedule. He managed the home front while I was doing things like driving to and from Laredo (four hours each way) to have lunch with a prospective client.

At the time, both J.C. and I were taking weekly allergy shots and there was a La Madeleine bakery near the doctor's office. Two cafe lattes and two croissants cost us $15 to $20 including tip. The next time we got our allergy shots and went to La Madeline for a snack, I was excited to tell J.C., "If we get black coffee and add our own milk, we can take a couple free slices of bread, and it will only cost us four dollars!" He turned to me with raised eyebrows and said, "Can you make four dollars today?" I frowned hard, knit my brow, and said no with a toddler sneer.

J.C. was right: Until we convinced clients to give us a chance, we would have no ability to put money in our pockets. To say nothing of needing to cover the company's costs (office rent and expenses, computers, administrative costs, etc.) before we took any pay home. We quickly learned about the canyon of time between signing a contract and getting paid.

My partners and I knew we had to get clients as soon as we moved into our office on Spicewood Springs Road. We started making phone calls. We created one-pagers listing our qualifications and reached out to all the firms we knew to tell them we'd hung out our shingle and were ready to work. We bought cheap but modern furniture from IKEA and an inexpensive coffee pot from Target. We cleaned the kitchen and bathroom ourselves — the unglamorous tasks of a startup.

We knew we would have to pitch ourselves to potential clients many times for any single opportunity. During the earliest days of our company in our small Spicewood Springs office, business was still done via phone call or business lunch, rather than Zoom or email. I would sit at my IKEA desk with my computer screen to my left and the landline telephone sitting in front of me. My business partners and I each had a contact list, and we diligently worked through the list, taking notes and reporting back. We would later say that we had no Plan B: Plan A was to succeed, come hell or high water.

That meant we "ran the roads" visiting past and potential clients with a marketing folder. We would ask people to call us in two weeks, two months, or two years. That unfolded for us in each of those timelines. To get contracts, we had to get on proposal teams to compete for work. When we sent out lists of project experience to potential teaming partners, we tabulated all the "Nos" but believed that at some point, we would get a "Yes." First, to be on a team, and later, to be on a winning team. A few months into hanging out our shingle, what ended up being a longtime client took a chance on us, and we completed what would become a long line of environmental studies for Texas infrastructure projects.

Fortunately, we gained clients' trust quickly — they'd worked with either me or Larry before, and they knew we did high-quality work. Some of those clients knew our costs would be lower and our desire to perform would be higher than our competitors. From the beginning, we never expected work to just walk in the door.

As our company grew, and we spread the word that CMEC was available to work, we repeated my dad's mantra: Win a few, lose a lot. In an increasingly crowded field of environmental consultants in the 2000s, and even of certified businesses (WBE/HUB/DBE firms), we appreciated each opportunity and knew we'd have to earn the next one. That ethic was a central motivator for the lifespan of CMEC.

For health and sanity, I took walks at lunchtime through the neighborhood to the small park at Stillhouse Hollow Nature Preserve. I knew there were endangered species living in the karst features of the park, and I was committed to protecting creatures like them by preparing City of Austin environmental compliance documents for clients. Exploring this park reminded me of childhood searches for tadpoles and doodle bugs in my backyard.

Generally, I'm an optimist, so I went to work with a positive attitude and the determination to succeed. But I recall one day feeling lightheaded, my heart beating out of my chest, and I had to lie down on the carpet. I feared I was having a heart attack, but the feeling passed. I imagine my body was panicking over taking such a huge risk. If it didn't work out, then my family would be behind on paying the mortgage, car insurance, and graduate school loan payments, to say nothing of savings to send the boys to college. I had feared financial insecurity since my parents' divorce. I got up off the floor, and it didn't happen again. I've since learned from my therapist that my "protector part" is overdeveloped and suppressed the great majority of my fear and trepidation down into the deepest recesses of my body. Ironically, in the early days of CMEC, my father offered solid advice for us, in addition to preparing articles of incorporation and bylaws, plus contracts and subcontracts that would serve our small company for years, mostly free of charge. Dad and I were comfortable with business-centered conversations. This helped us get into the black quickly.

One of our first jobs was conducting nighttime deer surveys for two different state agencies on several large properties they maintained. The deer surveys were part of wildlife management strategies. One person would drive, a second person would use the spotlight and binoculars to spot deer, and a third person would mark down how many deer and what type (doe, fawn, buck) we spotted. The best nights were when we could take our boys — mine plus Larry and Lorie's — along for the count. They loved riding in the back of the truck, calling out deer sightings (often inaccurately), and chomping Big League Chew to pretend they were dipping.

The most eventful night was in Brownwood, Texas. The property was huge, hilly, and wooded. We had seen bucks with large antler racks, Great Horned Owls, and a porcupine there. That particular night, we spotted a rare mountain lion just before heavy rain hit, which led to a tire blowout from a pair purchased that morning. Hours passed before we managed to contact a park ranger on the walkie-talkie, just as Larry finished replacing the tire. I was scared, but we finished the assignment and got home at dawn.

As a planner, most of my fieldwork involved exploring a project study area to understand what aspects of the community could be impacted if the transportation project were built. I identified existing land-uses, homes and businesses, and community facilities such as schools and churches. I assessed how peoples' views would change and documented "goat paths" indicating where the transportation agency should install a sidewalk.

The most satisfying technical victories came when our company was selected for contracts. We became the flavor of the day of environmental subcontractors for the Department of Transportation's project-specific and evergreen projects in the early 2010s. We repeatedly won the TxDOT Environmental Affairs (ENV) evergreen contract for years and provided a multitude of services all over Texas. We secured similar contracts in Oklahoma and developed a reputation for excellent cultural resources (archeological and architectural history work). As the prime contractor, we had to comply with Texas professional services procurement requirements and therefore brought in some team members as subcontractors.

My mother was an interior designer for many decades. She was beloved by her clients, committed to high quality work, and maintained relationships with some subcontractors for decades (wallpaper people, upholsterers, painters, a rug seller, and others). She always made sure she received their invoices in a timely manner and paid them promptly. That stuck with me as good business practice — your projects are only as good and fast as the slowest subcontractor. In our business, we often had to subcontract with a company with complementary skill sets. Take care of your subcontractors, and they'll take care of you.

A wise mentor told us it is relatively easy to have a small company, and somewhat easy to have a company once you bring on additional project managers (and people managers). But the "teenage years" are tough — the phase when we had between ten to forty employees. That's when the need for more scaffolding became evident — administrative capacity for invoicing and managing accounts, professional development training, human resources challenges, conflict resolution, and salary or benefits issues. In the early days, my business partners and I could holler to each other down the hall to coordinate. When the company grew larger, we found great leaders for different technical departments and geographic locations. But our mentor was right — the phase in between was tough. We had little to no ability to delegate management decisions. It was helpful to expect those growing pains.

Meanwhile, we were grooming and promoting staff from technical task leads to small project management roles, then to larger project management roles. One of my proudest moments was when a staff member said that working at CMEC gave him agency, demonstrating that management valued ideas and opinions from staff and truly wanted what was best for them. That sentiment motivated me to strive to be an authentic and supportive leader.

Exploring points of view in rural France, 1997.

Part IV: What We Build

We decided to commit to our community by purchasing a modest house with a hole in the floor. We chose to dig deeper roots in Austin and anchor our home and family there.

In 2000, we had our first child. Our siblings and parents joined us in Austin. Our village helped raise our boys — our second son arrived in 2003. These chapters are written from a bird's-eye view, but nothing shaped my life more profoundly than motherhood and meeting someone who looked like me.

My sister's choices separated us geographically and then brought us closer emotionally. To our surprise and delight, more family members moved to Austin, allowing our kids to grow up surrounded by a caring village of relatives.

After starting a company with two partners, I invested fifteen years of mental, emotional, and financial resources (to say nothing of elbow grease) into creating a successful business. My identity intertwined with my work in environmental stewardship. Then COVID hit, and the world stopped. Mortality forced reconciliation and reprioritization. And I thought about what it meant to be a gift.

Top: Our home, 1998. Bottom: Our home, 2025.

Our House Is a Very, Very, Very Fine House

Austin, 1998 – 2024

Once J.C. graduated from architecture school, he wanted to roll up his sleeves and physically work on our own house. We drove around on weekends looking for "sale" signs and getting a feel for different neighborhoods. We explored neighborhoods south of Town Lake. We were attracted to Zilker, Bouldin Creek, and Travis Heights, but we couldn't work with a Realtor until after J.C. got a full-time job, so we could determine our budget.

Meanwhile, we could finally go out together and enjoy what Austin had to offer. Work friends liked happy hour on 4th Street, which was emerging as a nightlife hub. J.C. and I ate at Jovita's on South 1st Street. (In 2012, Jovita's was busted for being a front for heroin operations, which sparked a slew of jokes about horse enchiladas and addictive hot sauce.)

On 2nd Street, Liberty Lunch was a large warehouse that hosted live music, and we attended many concerts there for cheap. Shady Grove restaurant was a staple in our social lives; Unplugged at the Grove was a free outdoor live music series where we could take a picnic blanket and relax on the Barton Springs Road lawn while enjoying chips and salsa with a margarita. We briefly considered moving back to San Francisco, but I had a good job. Also, we did the math and concluded we could buy a house in Austin and fly to San Francisco once a month for the same amount of money we would need to buy a house in the Bay Area, which was at the height of the dot-com boom. Many Stanford friends were getting tech jobs, and their compensation started including stock options. Several became wealthy quickly; other companies failed fast. J.C. and I felt traditional with our W-9 jobs in the old-fashioned fields of architecture and planning, but we were stable, content, and excited to house shop in earnest. I sang along in the car to my favorite song by Talking Heads, "This Must Be the Place (Naïve Melody)."

J.C. secured a full-time job working downtown at the office of Black & Vernooy. Sinclair Black was an urban design specialist who also taught at UT, and J.C. was excited to learn under his wing. I picked him up after work on 4th Street by pulling up to the curb and honking the car horn.

With our jobs locked in, we reached out to our friend Audrey to be our Realtor. She would fax MLS listings that met our criteria to my office. They came out of the machine on slick, curly paper, and I took them home to peruse with J.C. After visiting many houses, we almost put in an offer on a lovely house on Montclair Street. But it was too much of a stretch at $120,000.

I remember when we first drove up to a modest house on Wilson Street. It was a 850-square-foot cottage from the 1930s, white with red trim, asphalt shingles, and an iron railing on the porch. We didn't love that there was an institutional property catty-corner (Phoenix Academy moved in shortly after we bought our house; it was an inpatient and outpatient rehabilitation facility, which turned out to be a good neighbor for years). When we toured the house, it smelled terribly of cat urine. There was off-white, stained carpet, thin beadboard on the walls, a sprayed popcorn ceiling, and a bad kitchen renovation from the 1970s. We were told a hermit-like "computer type" had lived there; we imagined they never left the house.

But since it was built in 1935, it had good bones. It was pier-and-beam construction with large windows and a good flow from room to room. The backyard was lovely, with healthy grass growing under two gorgeous live oak trees. It would take some work, but we were up for it. J.C. was ready to own a house we could "take a hammer to." It was a financial leap, but with help from family, we scraped up the down payment for the $108,000 mortgage to move into the house. The porn theater three blocks away on South Congress and West Live Oak shut down right when we closed on the house.

After ending the lease on Maufrais Street, we had one week to work on the Wilson Street house before moving in. The August weather was sweltering and humid. After work each day, we headed over to make the house livable. To mask the horrible smell, we burned vanilla-scented candles in every room. We ripped out and threw away the stinking shag carpet and pried out the carpet nailing strips. We scraped the popcorn off the ceiling. J.C. broke open a wall while looking to relocate an electrical socket and discovered our ancient, fire-prone, knob-and-tube wiring. The previous owners had glued the carpet down, so we rented a floor

Left: Second major reconstruction of Wilson Street home designed by J.C. to better accommodate our growing sons. Right: Custom bookshelf in our dining room designed by J.C.

sander but failed to apply any kind of adhesive remover and ground down a few spots too much. Fortunately, the pine floors were thick enough to withstand our mediocre sanding and staining job, which we left up to professionals in subsequent renovations.

We used a heat gun to scrape off layers of paint (likely full of lead) in the wooden archway and painted over the faux wooden beadboard with bright colors. When we pulled up old bathroom tile, the fleas living in the floor leapt onto J.C.'s hairy legs. We listened suspiciously to frantic scurrying sounds in the creepy attic and called the exterminators. When the dishwasher broke, we pulled it away from the wall and saw rat carcasses underneath. After we cooked a frozen pizza in the oven, we found a mouse nest in the stove corner. Disgusted, we called in the home insurance policy and bought new low-cost appliances.

After that back-breaking week, the house was still a work in progress, but it was cleaner, freshly painted, and furnished with the essentials we needed. We were so excited to be homeowners.

We lived there cozily and learned to be parents when our first son arrived in 2000. We added on to the house in 2002, when our second son was on the way. We called it the stealth addition because it wasn't visible from the street: It included a new living room, plus a primary bedroom and bathroom added off the back of the house. We could give our old bedroom to the baby, so both boys were at the front of the house with their bathroom in between. We affixed a metal panel to the wall next to the bathtub so the boys could play with magnetic letters and animals during the sweet, fleeting years of bubble bath time. The updated front yard featured an aluminum glider and a tree swing made of a rubber tire in the shape of a horse that the boys named Silver.

In 2012, we reconstructed the home again, adding a second floor so our growing sons could have their own space. We rented the house across the street for the first months of that project while the kids were in school. I thought we were just remodeling but realized we were undertaking full reconstruction once the whole roof was ripped off. It was fascinating to see the layers of walls that captured the home's evolution — beadboard covered the fabric-backed wallpaper, which covered shiplap wood walls. J.C. specifically used salvaged shiplap to create the upstairs floors, which made me proud from a conservation and history perspective. With the boys in mind, J.C. designed a reading loft in their shared bedroom and a Scooby-Doo room hidden behind a bookshelf filled with the Hardy Boys series. It rolled back on skateboard wheels to reveal a music room where the boys played guitar and drums for a few blissful years. I loved hearing them play upstairs, regardless of the volume.

To comply with land use codes, we couldn't add floor area over the dining room, so J.C. designed a beautiful double-height space and tall bookshelf that lined the front wall of the house. Gables and dormers brought in light from upstairs, and it felt like living in a tree house. The front porch along the length of the house featured repurposed limestone tiles harvested from the UT LBJ Library renovation: J.C. had a contact who had been part of that job, so he provided us with the historic materials at a great price.

Sometimes it was stressful to be married to an architect, when the house was torn up, and I had to trust his vision while juggling work and parenting. During reconstruction, we temporarily stored large furniture but otherwise piled and stacked our things in the stealth addition. As the main house was finished out over the hot summer months, the boys slept in the living room, and the bathroom served double duty as the kitchen (the bitchen, as we called it).

After the work was done, we had a Christmas brunch and filled the house with friends and kids. I beamed with pride at the big landscape rocks in the front yard that provided access for climbing the green ash tree, while J.C. handed out mimosas and led the house tours. J.C.'s design work was honored when our home was selected for the 2012 Austin AIA Homes Tour and featured in a magazine.

Steamboat Springs lot on Alpenglow Way in 2021.

Hundreds of people came up the walk to explore the house. They wore poofy temporary booties, so as not to scuff the floors.

Our actual home — and our idea of home — continued to evolve, as we have. While imagining an escape to faraway lands during COVID, J.C. found a quarter-acre lot in Steamboat Springs, Colorado. It was cheaper than land in Austin, so we took a chance and purchased it so J.C. could design our first-ever, ground-up dream house. From 2021 to 2024, we collected art, furniture, books, paint and tile samples, wallpaper, and fabric swatches for the Colorado home. Wilson Street became cluttered and messy. Then, in May 2024, along with professional movers, we hauled all those items to Steamboat and started squatting in our own home, willing it to completion, despite being behind schedule and over budget.

Wilson Street also needed attention. We had the exterior repainted, and the house practically puffed up its gables and stood tall and proud. We painted the living room and primary suite walls a warm, soothing green. We rebuilt the primary bathroom and added black and white quartzite countertops, Japanese tile in the shower, and warm Sienna-colored cabinets. Upstairs, the boys' rooms became navy blue, and we replaced old soccer and rapper posters with art by friends. We had the staircase and kitchen walls repainted to cover the grime accumulated from years raising boys and dogs.

Lastly, we repainted the front lounge and the back office with handsome dark teal. We cleared out the kids' school supplies and stacks of papers everyone fears throwing away (we shredded bank statements, old bills, and insurance

Corner on Wilson street showing paintings by Vicki Schmeil and Granny Esther.

information, but kept birthday cards and love letters). We replaced the worn-out carpets and resurrected art from our parents' collections, interwoven with new art and original work by J.C.'s mom, Vicki, and my Granny Esther. The small collection of paintings in one corner above my mom's antique writing desk is a time capsule that honors our past. Several paintings hanging there show a house in various seasons. Writing this allowed me to slow down and appreciate the homes J.C. and I grew up in, along with the creative talents of the women who came before us. I feel fulfilled because our Austin home has provided warmth and stability for us and our sons all these years. Our Colorado home holds dreams of spending many days in the mountains with our children and their future families gathered around the table.

Meeting My First Blood Relatives and Parenting

Austin, 1999 – 2021

In 1999, J.C. and I felt like we were bona fide grown-ups. We had good jobs and a home. We were successfully raising our adopted puppy, Toba (named after the Sumatra Lake we had visited). It was the end of the millennium, which led to some existential thinking that year, alongside Prince's party song "1999" (released in 1982) playing constantly on the radio. People speculated about the year 2000 — centered around the fear that computer clocks couldn't handle the transfer to a new millennium because they were programmed with the last two digits of a year rather than all four digits. Would everything turn back to the year 1900 when the clock struck midnight? J.C. and I decided if the world went to hell in a handbasket, we would stock up on PowerBars and Gatorades and ride our bikes to Aunt Jeanne and Uncle Paul's ranch near Sealy, Texas, on the Brazos River. Generally, we disagree with their politics, but we all shared a mutual appreciation for land and natural resources. They had river access, water wells, and ample game. We could live off the land, if needed.

J.C. and I spent a romantic weekend around our November dating anniversary in Castroville, the Little Alsace of Texas. We discussed being ready to have kids. After all, it took my mother sixteen years to assemble her family (trying to conceive, adopting me, miscarrying, and then having Sloan). I'll never forget J.C. saying, "I hate to break it to you, but you're probably a Fertile Myrtle since you're adopted." I was surprised and amused to hear this. It was exciting to start trying to get pregnant after trying not to get pregnant for more than a decade. By Christmas, we succeeded.

That New Year's Eve, we went downtown with our friends David and Audrey. In a moment of regression, J.C. and David decided to streak across the Congress Avenue bridge, heading south wearing only their tennis shoes. I then told our friends it was good for the guys to get the immaturity out of their systems because

J.C. and I would soon be having a baby. Later that night, we toasted with Martinelli's sparkling cider and woke up to a normal world on January 1, 2000.

Meanwhile, J.C.'s brother and sister-in-law, Chris and Jennifer, moved to Austin. Chris had finished his residency in emergency medicine and got a job in Austin, which delighted us. Jennifer was a labor and delivery nurse, greatly helping me during my pregnancy. How fortunate we were to have medical professionals in the family. As a type A, controlling pregnant woman, I thought I could plan out how the actual birth would go. Luckily, Jennifer told me about the births she assisted with as a nurse. The more detailed the birth plan was, the further away the actual birth story unfolded. She helped me let go of the illusion of control; I would try natural birth but accepted the idea that I could change my mind and opt for an epidural part-way through labor. When my August due date arrived, Jennifer asked me to meet her for coffee at the arboretum. She sent me outside to jog around the outdoor pathway, since it was a Friday, and wouldn't it be great if Corbin was born on a weekend so my parents could visit from Dallas? J.C. procrastinated getting the car seat installed and packing his bag. When my water broke in the middle of the night on August 7th, J.C. sleepily said, "That's nice sweetie, go to sleep, and we'll call the doctor in the morning." I turned on the lights, ripped the covers off, and cussed loudly to wake him up and told him to hustle so we could head to the hospital.

After a long labor with Jennifer's assistance, on August 8, 2000, the Year of the Dragon, James Corbin McLain Schmeil was born at Renaissance Women's Center in Austin. When the doctors said, "It's a boy!" my dad, who had his ear to the door, said, "Oh, shit!" He feared for a boy born into a family dominated by women. I was delighted that the skinny, big-headed, gray-blue-eyed, bald baby boy was mine. For the first time in my life, I was seeing a blood relative. I was thrilled to watch him grow up. I have no memory of thinking about my biological mother at that moment — just my own selfish joy that we had created this beautiful child. Sure, he was a squooshy pink lump, but I knew he was 50 percent my genes, and I fell deeply in love.

After six weeks of unpaid maternity leave, other than accrued vacation and sick days, I returned to work from home a few days a week. I gradually increased from part-time to full-time back in the office over the course of a year with lots of help from J.C. At the same time, Corbin started attending Kids Are First on Enfield Road. We still have lifelong friends who we met when our kids were in daycare together.

Proud parents with my first known blood relative, James Corbin.

At that time, working from home meant taking printed documents to the house to mark up by hand or typing up public meeting documents and taking the files back to the office on a floppy disk, or later a hard disk (this was before CDs). I worked on the computer in our dark red, paneled dining room on my mom's small, antique desk. I worked in fits and starts, given the constant push and pull between needing to work and needing to sleep when the baby slept. My mom was a true blessing as she cooked, cleaned, and helped care for our son, but we were on our own after she returned to Dallas.

The first couple years of the new millennium were one big brain fog for me. Corbin did not sleep through the night for the first two and a half years of his life, but like many women, I plowed ahead and worked my sleep-deprived ass off anyway. I worked hard at Hicks & Company and did my best to be a good mother, though I made plenty of mistakes, like leaving a tiny rock in my son's head for two weeks thinking it was a scab; children forge ahead on their own strength when they see us do the same. With J.C.'s flexibility at his architecture practice, he and I juggled household duties.

The one clear memory I have from that period is September 11, 2001. Our world changed forever just after Corbin's first birthday. I remember the exact details of that day — in particular, the sadness of the daycare workers when I picked up Corbin. We were all nervous for the unclear future for the children. I immediately feared for mothers and their sons who might have to go to war. Somehow, we all moved forward.

By late 2002, we were ready to start trying to get pregnant again. We needed more space, so J.C. designed our stealth addition, adding a living room and primary suite to the back of our house. Once we were dried in, we got pregnant again easily.

While I was busy working and parenting, my due date came up quickly, and Corbin — miraculously — started sleeping just in time. For my second child, my birth plan was just a copy of the original birth plan for Corbin, marked up with new dates written in a green metallic Sharpie. Like Jennifer tried to teach me during my first pregnancy, parenting repeatedly teaches one crucial lesson to parents: Get over yourself and the illusion of control. After another long labor, this time at North Austin Medical Center, Thomas Beckett McLain Schmeil was born on March 1, 2003, which happened to be his Uncle Chris' birthday. We gave Corbin a stuffed dinosaur in the hospital, and he gave his new baby brother a smaller stuffed dinosaur of his own.

As they grew, both boys had blue eyes with blond hair. Beckett's hair was curlier, like J.C.'s, and his eyebrows were darker. Corbin's brows and lashes were white and would stay that way. I was delighted to stare into their little faces searching for some resemblance to me: They had my hair and fair skin. Did they have my nose or J.C.'s? Would they be athletic like J.C. or flexible like me? Would they be musical like me? Witty like J.C.? I wondered how we would see our genes manifest in our sons — probably a bit more than mothers who can see themselves in their parents.

My second unpaid maternity leave was a blur. Since Corbin had been a terrible sleeper, my mom insisted on a strict schedule for Beckett. We were open to Beckett having a pacifier — anything he wanted to become attached to so I could sleep. He eventually accumulated a pacifier, a silk pillowcase, a blanket, and a stuffed guinea pig that he later named Stubby to help him sleep. We joked we would have allowed him cigarettes if it meant we could rest. Fortunately, Jerry and Vicki, my in-laws, had moved to nearby Lakeway and played a critical support role for our kids and all the Schmeil cousins.

Both Corbin and Beckett attended Travis Heights Elementary School in our 78704 neighborhood and went on to attend public schools in Austin Independent School District (AISD) through graduation. The school was socioeconomically diverse, but in truth, this meant lots of neighbors with graduate degrees, many others with lower economic status, and not much in the middle. We loved the teachers and the community — so many great parents who are still our friends,

Corbin and Beckett on a summer trip to visit Schmeil family in Seattle.

committed to public schools and to the eclectic group of neighborhood kids served by the school under the live oak trees. The school had a special spirit and strong leadership. Friday pep rallies were rock concerts, with teachers playing instruments and kids dancing to "Thunderbirds Really Rock!" Beckett had a chance to play in a kid band at Travis Heights and felt like a star.

I pulled from my professional networks to expose students to science careers by organizing Young Scientists' Day when we filled the school with volunteer scientists: archaeologists, doctors, forensic investigators, and herpetologists. Young Scientists' Day was the one day of the year I felt valuable as a parent in the school community, rather than the mom who primarily served as a breadwinner. I was passionate about creating exposure to the sciences for the neighborhood kids, and my kids were able to understand the importance of my work and science in general. I worked a lot when the boys were young, especially when I started Cox|McLain Environmental Consulting.

Years later, when Corbin was writing about memories for a high school class, he talked about remembering a summer day camp. In his story, he said he and his brother were usually the last ones to get picked up by me — ouch. But he didn't mind staying late because the younger kids could watch the older kids play video games. I was shocked at the specificity of memories he wrote about and saddened by the assertion, though small, that my work demands had consequences. At the time, I was trying to launch my company and cram as much as I could into my workday so I could focus on the kids at home, but I was prone to finishing just

Beckett in 9th grade, Corbin in 12th.

one more thing before getting in the car for the commute to pick up the boys from camp.

Thankfully, J.C. was always there for the daily routine — carpool, school, and sports on repeat. J.C. supported our sons academically. He not only showed up, but he also coached baseball, basketball, football, and soccer. The busier I got at work, the more he stepped up, including becoming the family dinner chef.

Both boys attended Kealing, a math- and science-focused magnet middle school in East Austin. The school had interesting elective courses, such as animal studies and World War II through film. In addition to sports, Corbin played saxophone through high school. Beckett had a short stint on clarinet, then some creative rock-and-roll time with We Love Music in a band called the Neons, until he branched off and started composing his own music on the computer and guitar.

Corbin and then Beckett were admitted to the selective high school, the Liberal Arts and Science Academy (LASA). LASA was a magnet program that shared a building with LBJ High School. LASA offered great electives, from fashion design to astronomy, and stellar teachers. Core courses were rigorous and created an excellent foundation that would serve the boys in future academics. Both boys played Elite Club National League soccer on traveling teams. The hours and dollars spent both kept them physically healthy and taught them how to win and how to lose.

J.C. and I did our best to support their activities, attending games and music performances while teaching the boys to drive and develop personal agency. They both held summer jobs, either tutoring or in the service industry. Both spent time doing admin or landscaping work for CMEC — a smart idea from our college financial advisor who helped us recognize we could put our kids on the payroll to earn their allowance while reducing our tax burden.

Corbin is a classic first-born child — responsible, academically strong, organized, and respectful. He isn't shy but introverted and satisfied with his small group of quality friends. When he was admitted early action to Stanford, J.C. and I were elated. Always cautious and thorough, Corbin waited until the last 24 hours before the deadline to accept admission and decide to attend.

Corbin started Stanford in the fall 2018 after a family trip to Italy. He had nice roommates, rode his bike all over campus, and played club soccer. He studied hard and did well in his classes. Winter quarter sophomore year, Corbin got a chance to try a blind-folded free throw from center court at a Stanford basketball game — he made it and won $500. In March, he and a friend headed to Tahoe to ski. They skied for one day before the news hit that the world was being slammed by a pandemic of coronavirus, or COVID-19.

Everyone has a COVID story, and we are the same. Corbin packed an overnight bag and flew home for less than $100. Little did he know, he wouldn't be able to get back on campus for fourteen months. He and friends tried a remote study stint in Seattle that coincided with forest fires there, resulting in an anxiety-inducing, mixed-bag experience.

Beckett is a creative spirit, extroverted, less predictable, and more of a risk taker. He remains curious, smart, creative, and resourceful. He learned music theory, songwriting, and computer music skills at LASA. He took fashion design and modeled in a show. He was on track to have an excellent senior year when COVID hit.

My work COVID story posed immense challenges. But having Corbin home from Stanford and having Beckett taking classes remotely while J.C. and I both worked from home turned out to be a gift. For that period, I stopped commuting on MoPac, sitting in traffic, eating in the car, rushing out of the house. I exercised and had coffee on the back patio. I wrote in my journal, took a class on the science of happiness, and stared up at the live oaks, saying to myself, "Reach and branch." We adopted our second puppy, Siena, and passed her around to cuddle. The boys learned to cook. They spent time together. Stuck at home, we bonded.

Corbin studied Italian for a year but never felt comfortable accepting the offer to attend the Florence program for fear of another COVID breakout. Finally, he returned to Stanford for spring quarter junior year, driving a Honda Pilot I gave him so he would have mobility and freedom after the lockdowns, and life started to normalize. He embarked on the much more enjoyable half of his career at Stanford.

Junior year of high school, Beckett was on track to get recruited to play college soccer. He was pursued by several small Division 3 universities. COVID was rampant, so college visits were strange, requiring masks and outdoor-only tours. He had some bad luck — he missed a recruiting camp when he mysteriously contracted mono. He broke his wrist in basketball practice and missed some soccer games. Lonestar club soccer continued, but many games were canceled, and the travel no longer seemed worth it. Overall, Beckett wasn't looking forward to senior year, when he would be stuck taking challenging LASA AP classes remotely.

The only thing he looked forward to was playing basketball. The new coach came on when LASA and LBJ split up athletics for UIL a year before LASA and LBJ became physically separate schools. The boys received new navy and white uniforms and became the LASA Raptors. With the talented LBJ basketball players now on a separate team, Beckett and pals rose to become stars of the LASA basketball team, in addition to playing on the LASA soccer team. The coach taught the boys to treat each other like family, to support each other, and to grow as young men, not just to win. When he realized he wanted camaraderie more than competition, and that he knew he needed to make the right choice for himself (not for his parents), Beckett scrapped the idea of soccer being his ticket to college.

The morning after, he came downstairs to tell us he was applying to the most beautiful colleges he could find, including Elon University in North Carolina, which had about 6,600 students — a great size — located on a 600-acre botanical garden maintained by the state of North Carolina. Beckett applied in the fall, received early admission, and enjoyed a quiet but encouraging campus tour in February. Assuming the world would recover from COVID, Elon had great overseas programs, which attracted Beckett. In the final weeks of college decision time, his childhood friend Charlie was admitted and, after his visit, was convinced about Elon, too. This meant all of us, including Charlie's parents, Jann and Randy, some of our best friends to this day, could road trip together to drop the boys, their cars, and their guitars in North Carolina in fall 2021.

It is impossible to capture the story of parenting two remarkable young men in a few pages. Motherhood has been my most fulfilling job, and my two boys have been miraculous and precious to me since their arrival. These few highlights of

Top: Celebrating Beckett's Elon graduation with family.
Bottom: Corbin's master's graduation.

my motherhood journey have brought me joy because at times, I feared my workaholic tendencies created distance between us or meant I fell short as a mom. A positive byproduct of my work has been that J.C. and the boys share a love of athletics and healthy competition. I humbly attribute their cooking skills and attention to fashion to their father. My partnership with J.C. is solid, and our sons have not experienced divorce. They did not have to change schools growing up. We have chosen to live where they have been surrounded by family — aunts, uncles, cousins, grandparents. Our village on Wilson Street in Travis Heights gave them stability and a strong foundation from which to launch into the world.

Top: McLain Wait Dockery family sailing in the BVI, 2009. Bottom: Schmeil cousins in Carcassonne, France: Thompson, Beckett, Anna, Lucy, and Corbin.

Shaping Our Families

2000 – Present

My mother and J.C.'s parents highly valued sharing their love of travel with us. I enjoyed Vicki and Jerry's stories of living overseas. Once I had my two boys, I aimed to follow Vicki's example of taking them anywhere and everywhere we could. When I was a young mother, I remember friends saying, "We're going to wait to travel until our kids are older, so they'll remember it." Not us.

J.C. has memories of nearly all the places he's lived except Switzerland, since he was only two. He remembers being wrapped up in warm clothes, gloves, and hats to play outside in the dark when he lived in Stockholm from ages three to five. He lived in Côte d'Ivoire, West Africa, from age five to eight and has many exciting and dramatic stories involving monkey poop, crocodiles and raw chicken, and fending off insects. When Corbin was born, J.C.'s parents lived in Singapore, and the next year, my sister Sloan moved to Thailand. So, we had an excuse to travel.

In 2001, my sister was living in Chiang Mai, Thailand, teaching English. She was deeply respected there, as were all teachers. She started telling us about spending time with a guy. She sent pictures and told us about their road trips. He was an antique dealer, and Sloan traveled with him throughout Thailand searching for vases, sculptures, and artifacts he could refurbish and sell.

Though we thought her time overseas would be an adventure or a short stint, my sister decided to marry and have a baby. At that time, J.C.'s parents weren't too far away in Singapore, and J.C. had grown up in Tokyo, so I assumed we would visit as often as possible. Mom, J.C., Corbin, and I flew through Tokyo, spent Christmas there, then continued on to Thailand.

Corbin's passport featured his ten-week-old photo (me holding him against the wall for the photo in his onesie, my arms outstretched). He didn't even have baby fat yet. We originally got it to visit J.C.'s parents in Singapore when Corbin was four months old. By the time we were heading to Thailand for my nephew's birth, Corbin was a busy, chatty toddler with a large head and a little strip of blonde hair at the nape of his neck, like Grandpa Munster.

Corbin and I meeting an elephant in Chiang Mai, Thailand.

We arrived in Tokyo, lit with holiday lights amidst the neon of Roppongi, and explored J.C.'s former neighborhood haunts. We went to a church on Christmas Day and stayed in a traditional hotel with tatami mats. While J.C., Mom, and I slept on the mats, Corbin tumbled over our sleeping bodies and put a hand through the thin shoji screen wall.

We continued to Chiang Mai with a layover in Bangkok. We made it through the 30-hour flight. We thought we'd be there for Thana's birth, expected on Christmas Day, but he was born two weeks earlier on December 12th. We were delighted to see Sloan and meet her precious dark-haired, half-Thai son. The first night, we ate out at an exciting Thai market. We loved the pork balls so much that we took the leftovers back to store in our hotel mini fridge. Corbin got food poisoning and spent the night in the hospital getting top-notch care for a total of $40.

We visited tourist sights, ate wonderful meals, and explored their neighborhood. We sang Thai karaoke (or tried) and laughed until we cried; baby and toddler slept on our laps while we crooned to mystery tunes with unrelated videos. We watched elephants walk down the street. We attended a river festival where paper lanterns were lifted by candlelight up into the dark night sky, like a tiny fleet of explorer ships launching into the unknown.

When Sloan returned to the US in early 2003, she and Thana stayed with us. Once Beckett reached six weeks old, Sloan and toddler Thana moved in and slept on the futon in the front room. J.C. would take Corbin to daycare, and Sloan and I would alternate caring for Beckett and Thana or working. I did my usual consulting work, shouldering more project management experience. My sister looked for

Left: "Mimi" and "Dewey" Schmeil with Corbin in Singapore. Right: With Mom, Sloan, and baby Thana in Thailand.

work, apartments, and applied for a teaching program. We shared care for about six exhausting but fulfilling weeks.

Once Beckett reached three months old, he joined Corbin at daycare full-time, I returned to work full-time, and Sloan and her son moved into their own apartment where she crammed to pass the Texas Region 13 accelerated teaching certificate program. Sloan became certified to teach in Austin ISD (she recently celebrated twenty years with the district). Once she secured a teaching job, Sloan and son moved into a tiny house in lovely Hyde Park.

Happily, in 2005, she met Julian, an affable, smart, solid man from Liverpool and a recently divorced father of a beloved son and daughter who were a bit older than my nephew. They embarked on life together and set an incredible example for me about how to raise kids through adolescence — her stepson Sam and stepdaughter Alejandra were both older than Corbin, hence my younger sister became my parenting advisor. We cherish that our sons and these cousins grew up together in Austin.

Though we live in different cities, my mom, aunt, and my maternal cousins do our best to stay connected. Mom and Aunt Jeanne have been excellent professional role models for me and my sister in our careers. This family strength and resilience is buoyed by levity. Occasionally, we take what we call "Girly Girl" trips, where we eat and drink too much and laugh so hard we have tears streaming down our faces. Truly, humor has helped all of us make it through some really hard times. Like many families, we have been through (in no order and without attribution): divorce, cancer, addiction, job loss, financial chaos, adoption, suicide, abuse, betrayal . . . also education, land ownership, parenthood, new love, renewal, faith, joy, happiness, and success. Above all, we know the importance of family; we support each other as best we can; we share quotes to live by; and we share our heartfelt belly laughs as often as possible, alongside our tears. This is the legacy I have carried into my expanded family role from mother, daughter, and sister to wife, sister-in-law, daughter-in-law, and aunt.

We've been lucky to have J.C.'s family close by as well. Since brother- and sister-in-law Chris and Jennifer moved to Austin, their three kids Anna, Thompson, and Lucy have also grown up in Texas alongside our boys. Anna was born a year and a half after Corbin, and Thompson was born just five months after Beckett. I loved being part of the family support team when the kids were born, driving Jennifer to the hospital if Chris was working in the ER, or watching the babies with Vicki and Jerry while Jennifer's mom traveled from North Carolina to help. I had the privilege of witnessing my niece Lucy's birth. She was a towheaded blonde who I liked to carry on my hip at our holiday parties, pretending she was my daughter. Though the cousins went to different schools, we've shared birthdays, sporting events, celebrations, and holidays whenever we could.

Family is fundamental to all of us. Though we are different in many ways, we recognize the bonds we share — biological or not, geographically together or apart. The first cousins, in due time, dispersed for college — Washington State, California, Missouri, Pennsylvania, North Carolina, and Texas. They have all traveled or studied in various places outside the US, enriching their world views beyond the borders of our home city, state, and country. I hope our sons and all our nieces and nephews know they are valued and know we are cheering them on to become their most authentic selves as they face the trials and tribulations, sorrows, joys, and blessings that life will surely bring them.

Baptism by Fire and Letting Go

2017 – 2023

In the heyday of CMEC, we became busy with projects but had little time to prepare proper training manuals. I wrote a memo called "baptism by fire" that became an official part of the new employee onboarding materials. Later, we pulled in various service providers to help with administrative and human resources tasks that could be outsourced from CMEC. The best advice we received from hiring a management consulting company on our ten-year anniversary: We should invest in our second level of leadership because they'd be the focus of any strategic acquisition. That move strengthened our company. The same year, we moved the company headquarters into an office my business partners, myself, and my husband purchased and refurbished as an LLC on Shoal Creek Boulevard.

Starting in 2017, we doubled the size of our leadership team. They helped us get serious about tracking key performance indicators, getting time sheets submitted and invoices out the door and paid, tracking quality assurance/quality control documentation, building skill sets with intentional learning and growth efforts, and training more people on how to do marketing. Between 2017 and 2020, we had some of our best years. Our second-level leaders became stronger; our managers for our five offices were solid professionals; and we kept earning work from new and repeat clients.

My business partner was direct. It was true that we worked hard to build our standing, and the competitors in our field were just waiting for us to stumble and tarnish our good reputation. Hence, we developed a mantra of three tiers of quality control reviews (peer review, technical review, and project manager review) that had to be completed prior to submitting reports to clients. In Larry's words, if you put one turd on the table, you're done. Hard to get that effective image out of one's head.

A substantial amount of my work included public involvement support. Historically, the National Environmental Policy Act (NEPA) is invoked when federal dollars are spent on a project. The public is invited to review a project design, routes that are compared in an alternatives analysis, financial plans, and construction timelines. I genuinely cared about the public's thoughts about a project and helped people understand the purpose for the project (reducing traffic accidents, for example). I gained useful information from listening to people in the community — when they explained their flooding issues, or told me the location of an unmarked grave, or taught me that a church slated for relocation held services in three different languages.

I was pleased when we made agreements to mitigate adverse impacts to community members. What I didn't see often, due to the long timelines, was mitigation actually being completed. Mitigation measures may be prescribed as a condition of environmental clearance to put an infrastructure project out for bids for construction. Examples include noise walls; relocation of people, businesses, or community facilities with the intention of retaining some intact community fiber; wetland protection; or endangered species preservation. I invested a good deal of faith that mitigation would happen, and that it would work. It's still difficult for me to admit that, since it's rarely tracked after project construction, mitigation may be an unfulfilled promise of NEPA compliance.

Technology was always an uphill battle. We promised our staff we would obtain quality tools for them to get their work done. Over fifteen years, we led our company through the changes from physical maps to digital maps, landlines to cell phones, desktop computers to laptops, on-premises to cloud-based servers with all the associated security challenges. From day one, we worked with IT contractors to create triplicate backups for all our documentation.

The largest challenge occurred in May 2020 when a server crashed, and we lost our backups. We started intensely scrambling, cursing, and giving Herculean efforts to retrieve useful backup data. Ultimately, we permanently lost about three days of data. This meant we had to pay people overtime and out of pocket to redo fieldwork, rewrite reports, and resubmit deliverables. It helped us survive the nightmare to roll up our sleeves and fix what was lost. That server crash and recovery demonstrated the quality of staff working for CMEC, as well as the leadership direction provided by our management team to support them through that event. No one quit over the incident, even though this IT "nuclear event" occurred in the middle of the COVID lockdown. Sometimes, you just get back up after you're knocked down.

The biggest, most complex tasks I led were major highway widening projects or routing studies for brand new highways in or around large urban areas. For one large urban project executed by a large technical team (rebuilding Interstate 35 through Austin), I wrote a supplemental transportation equity and access analysis using a new technical tool that collected GPS-based data on bicycle and pedestrian movements across the major highway. My observations and opportunities storyboard highlighted places where heavily used sidewalks could be improved with shade structures, benches, or other simple assets that could beneficially impact lives. That study was a key reason the project received an innovative transportation solutions award from WTS International. I hope to see some of the human-serving components of the project realized.

The transit projects I worked on in Dallas, San Antonio, Houston, and Austin were near and dear to my heart because great urban areas can only become stronger when mobility is improved for driving and non-driving populations. This complex work challenged and motivated me on a professional and personal level. (I still harbor hope for light rail in Austin.)

When the company was smaller, it was easy for us three founders to play distinct roles, though we didn't name them until later. I became CEO — the outward-facing persona of the company. Lorie was COO — handled everything operational to get us and the staff paid. Larry was CFO — always concerned with the bottom line. He was great about telling staff to call their contacts, help us drum up business, and identify new market opportunities (new geographies, newly protected species such as bats or mussels, or new industries, such as renewables). When you're busiest, that's when you need to market the most. We had some slower years, but fortunately, year after year we profited — even during COVID. Still, as the company grew, it was harder to manage the challenges that came with growth, not only contractually, but also in terms of quality assurance/quality control, people management, professional development, and accountability. Also, and inevitably, the younger generation bonded and socialized, and the "boss" was no longer invited. At those times, being a leader could be lonely.

Managing people was a blessing and a curse. The more people you have, the more likely you'll get a mix of personalities. At our largest, we were 100 people, including archeology contractors, across five offices. The wonderful people were the reason to go to work every day. They had technical passions, new approaches, and entrepreneurial ideas. But the problem employees drained energy and kept me up at night. There was the cocky ecologist who completed exactly half of the required field work. During the early days of COVID, there were people who ghosted us. A couple of employees were bullies, a few were just irresponsible. One employee was let go after using a company card to take clients to a strip club and post a bail bond. In retrospect, we were often slow to act, and it was a relief each time we let someone go — it was never without justification.

With twenty-twenty hindsight, we should have acted sooner with several employees. If complaints were coming in about someone's behavior or how they were treating others, that issue would've been prioritized and dealt with quickly. Sometimes though, the issue wasn't black and white, and leaders formed differences of opinion. One case caused tension between managers because they didn't agree. Ultimately, we let one person go by managing them out, giving them time to find another position, and let them control the narrative of why they were leaving. We weren't surprised when the other party left the company anyway, though we took their side officially. We messaged this to staff as "irreconcilable differences" and ended up with better fits for the jobs.

Overall, we had excellent employees who were truly experts in their fields. We cared for our people well, offering merit bonuses, benefits, professional development, and promotions. Several staff members lost parents or other family members over the years; we always told them family comes first and to come back when they were ready. We had people's backs when they needed medical, parental, or bereavement leave. This meant employees became even more enthusiastic about working for us and, in turn, had the backs of their coworkers in times of need.

We made a great acquisition of Prewitt and Associates cultural resources experts in January 2020. We had just modernized their computer system and added them to our server when COVID hit. We pivoted quickly thanks to already having VPN technology for remote work (driven by field work). Larry, Lorie, and I focused on keeping people safe and then staying solvent, in that order. Our work was connected to infrastructure projects supported by the Bipartisan Infrastructure Law and deemed "essential services," allowing us to implement safe health practices while continuing to work and bring in income. But it was very stressful. The differences in our management styles were exacerbated by remote work, public health debates, and the political climate. Our staff members had various opinions about evolving health protocols and many of them contracted COVID in the early days before vaccines were approved. As we worked through that and through the server failure, we recognized we needed more scaffolding to support our growing company and to shoulder some of our burdens. We needed to move forward with our exit strategy.

After half a year working with my business partners to secure and evaluate options for an external sale of our company, we aligned and reached a decision. We had signed a letter of interest with one company that was acquired by a larger company the next week and were in the midst of an intensive corporate due-diligence process (we called it the Texas Two-Step). We set a date to tell our second level of leadership and then our staff. I was nervous: I feared my staff would feel tricked or betrayed. I spoke with my yoga teacher, who I'd known for years and who knew me well but not professionally. I told her I was concerned about what my staff would think. She looked me in the eye. I expected her to tell me to meditate, or breathe, or something similar. To my surprise she said, "Ashley, they're grown-ass adults, and you are not their mother." This shocked me at first, then made me laugh. She was right.

Most of our employees knew we had reasons for the decision. They witnessed our interactions over the years and knew how stressful it was to steer a company through COVID. I also mustered up courage for the sale announcement by speaking with my HiPower professional women's network colleagues. They told me to do what was right for me, regardless of whether others supported my decision. The advice from years earlier to be irreverent helped me make the decision to sell my company and take my name off the sign out front.

Despite developing a multitude of personal relationships through work, the business decision was clear. It was time to close the chapter on CMEC and pass the business along to the next generation of leaders. They needed the support and larger geographical and technical range that the acquiring company provided. Every one of our employees was retained and each of them could take their future in their own hands: They could stay, give the new company a chance, and identify a new personal growth path. Or they could leave.

We had holiday parties each year. Some offices held holiday-themed games and white elephant gift exchanges. Even in 2020, we had a remote trivia party and mailed treats to employees. Some of the most fun, relaxed, and meaningful moments came from connecting with staff across our offices. I always included photos in the annual reports; they captured the life and personality of the healthy business we created.

In 2021, I worked hard to plan a great party at a lively location but had a pit in my stomach. The following week, we'd tell the staff we had sold to a strategic acquirer. At the party, only our three other principals and a senior admin knew about the deal and were under nondisclosure agreements.

We had one last holiday party in Austin after our acquisition. At Austin's Easy Tiger on East 6th Street, Christmas 2022, I gave a brief speech. I talked about how grateful we were for everyone rallying through COVID and for the transition and integration into the larger company. I was proud of what we had all done together, that company founders had wanted a larger stage, more project locations, and more professional development for staff, and we believed the acquiring company was on track to provide that. The three founders no longer represented a professional ceiling. We were proud to take the scary, bold step of giving up our company name for expanded opportunities for staff.

The toasts were cautious that year, but you can't tell that from the pictures. We have a great group photo, including the former Prewitt and Associates staff members who constituted some of the strongest, most loving, and adaptable employees. The room was full of people with silly sweaters and broad smiles, grateful for coming through to the other side of COVID. But they were also protecting themselves. I could feel in the room that I had become separate from my people. I don't begrudge anyone for begrudging me — us — for deciding to sell the company. It was a huge change for everyone and the first year of integration was exhausting.

I would later learn there wasn't much room for personality to poke through a polished corporate veneer: The demands and responsibilities of a publicly traded company don't allow for that. Still, I have no doubt our business decision was a good one. I have no regrets.

Top: Last CMEC holiday party before the announcement of acquisition.
Bottom: OKC displaying holiday spirit.

I miss CMEC's staff happy hours on the deck beside Shoal Creek. We had the deck built to encourage people to take breaks by the waterway. We bought small foldable tables and chairs that anyone could carry if they wanted to eat lunch outside. We got a cranking umbrella that could be opened and angled to block the sun. We had anniversary parties outside where we presented long-term employees with a YETI cooler filled with their favorite beverages. One Halloween potluck was held outside, and we stood around dressed as witches, butterflies, and bats.

In winter, we'd watch a pair of Red-Tailed Hawks fly between bare branches hunting the small snakes and fish slithering along in the creek. I often took breaks outside and called family to check in while strolling along the creek. Sometimes on Sunday mornings, I worked inside and threaded a power cord out the window so my sons could landscape the creek slope. It was on weekends that I carefully hung photos in the hallways. At first, they were cheaply framed nature photos from my or my business partners' vacations. Then the collection expanded to photos of birds, spiders, owls, bluebonnets, archaeological trenches, or historic homes taken by our staff. I hung them up proudly to reflect our work and to remind all of us that our primary focus was to protect the environment.

After we sold our company, and I worked hard to fulfill the responsibilities of the regional business leader role at our acquiring company, I realized the job was not the right fit. The region was too large — nine Gulf states — and the charge was to manage staff from a productivity and profit perspective, not a role I'd been trained for. I wanted to connect with people and support them. I met with more than 200 people out of the 400+ in the region, but that wasn't the focus of the job, which put me at a crossroads. I could shrink my sphere of influence by going back to just working on projects in Texas, I could go back to being a project manager rather than being in a leadership role, or I could go where I was appreciated.

We had excellent timing for our acquisition, so I no longer needed to be rewarded with a paycheck or promotions. After soul-searching, I decided to be irreverent by focusing on my family and friends and directing my energy toward creative and philanthropic pursuits. In 2023, I followed my own advice by retiring.

My thirty-year environmental career ended on November 1, 2023. On that day, I started writing to look back at my life so I could gain perspective and understanding to carry into the future.

New Year's Day 2022 — checking building after a freeze; and putting on a brave face to steer our company through integration.

Steps up to our ever-evolving Austin home.

Stepping Up: Ode to Home

Wilson Street, 1998 – Present

"Good girl, good boy," I say to our dogs as we step up the curb in front of the Wilson Street home where we've lived for 27 years. We made it around the short walk without our fearful COVID dog Siena having too many freak-outs, and with our older dog Shiner stopping dozens of times to mark and re-mark his territory. How many times have I stepped up onto this walkway to our front door? Too many to count.

In 1998, we brought home our first pup, Toba. He was a reddish-brown, half Lab, half Rhodesian Ridgeback, with a black face and a huge heart. We walked him around the neighborhood full of charming cottages and baby strollers, occasionally spotting Leslie — our friendly, iconic South Austin cross-dresser wearing a Hooters outfit. Toba bounded up from the street, onto the walkway, and up onto the porch until we had to lift him up in our arms and carry him for his last few months in 2011.

We brought home baby Corbin in 2000 in the August heat, our homemade, street-front landscaping choking and withering in the heat. I carried baby Beckett, and my husband held Corbin's hand as we walked up that walkway in 2003 into our child-rearing-equipment-filled, newly expanded house. We took many evening walks with the kids — in front packs, then strollers, wagons, small bicycles with training wheels.

For more than twenty-five years, we welcomed our Travis Heights/Bouldin Creek neighbors and their families for the holidays. We were inspired by the Fezziwigs from *A Christmas Carol*, sharing the spirit of the holidays with dozens of people we loved. Our holiday parties featured elaborate appetizer plates, alcoholic drinks, and juice boxes. In-laws brought dozens of hand-decorated cookies on tiered trays. One year, the boys had so many Nerf sword wars that the front yard looked like the Renaissance Faire.

After our house reconstruction in 2012, we created a bedroom and bathroom called the "Grandsuite" for Mom, whom we call Grandsue, and who was visiting frequently while exploring a move to Austin. She was so excited to help with the colors — "Aunt Becky Blue" on the walls (after our eccentric, faux aunt in Galveston), warm gray for the bedding, bright red for the recovered chair donated from her collection in the corner next to the upright piano she'd secured from a Dallas neighbor. I can see Mom beaming with a glass of sauvignon blanc and a big book on her lap under the reading lamp.

In spring 2013, we first guided our rescue puppy, Shiner, up the walkway and into our home. He was four months old, fostered with police German Shepherds, potty trained, and very sweet. His big dark eyes, soft jet-black fur, and white chest, paw, and tail tip had us besotted from the beginning. Corbin said we couldn't keep his foster name, Shiner Bock, after the beer, but we stuck with Shiner because it suited him.

Christmas morning in 2016, Corbin opened his stocking to find a set of car keys, and he bolted out the front door, down the porch steps, and straight to the curb where the little black Honda CR-V sat parked with fuzzy dice hanging from the mirror. *Be safe, boys. Please, please come home in one piece.* How many times have I awakened at 3 a.m. and rushed on tiptoe to look with blurry eyesight out the front window, to see if their cars are parked there on the curb, meaning they are safely in their beds?

Many times, I walked down the porch steps and off the curb and gave my sons bear hugs, checked their gas tanks, made sure they had their AAA cards and cell phone chargers and could see out the back window over their belongings for their road trips back to college for the year, west to California and east to North Carolina.

I often hosted the book club I helped found in 1997. Fondly known as the Goddess Collective, a dozen long-time Austin women shared a love of literature, food, wine, and conversation. The chatty ladies stepped up onto the front walkway carrying a potluck dish, a dog-eared book, and a bottle of wine. Inside, we stood around the kitchen island snacking and chatting, then we retired to the living room to drink more, eat chocolate, and discuss the book and family and work challenges. I always felt warm and full, physically and spiritually, when we hugged at the front steps, and they dispersed to their cars to head home.

Our closest friends stepped up the sidewalk with Spanish cheese, birthday balloons, tiny cowboy hats, board games, growlers of beer, and their favorite wines. We sat around the dining room table playing songs on the record player, comparing stories, sharing laughter, popping corks, smudging glasses, and dirtying dishes.

When our whole family hunkered down in the house to wait out the COVID pandemic in 2020, we adopted Siena from Austin Pets Alive and carried her up the sidewalk and into the house with her fancy bed, food, and toys to present her to big brother Shiner for inspection.

When my dad moved to town in 2022, I brought back from his former office a bronze sculpture of a cowboy on horseback and a box of dusty books, including a 1926 version of *Billy the Kid.* When Parkinson's took over his body faster than his mind, we drove up to the curb and scurried over to the passenger side to help him out of the car. We'd get his walker out of the back seat. With his hulking frame leaning on that wiry walker, he pulled his scuffed rubber-soled shoes along the walkway by the force of stubborn will. He struggled up the steps with me and my sister on either side: walker first, one foot, then the next foot; walker, one foot, next foot. Once we got him seated at the dinner table, he told us stories about representing the little guy in his law practice, including a tale about the family member who died shortly after slipping on an errant lipstick tube at the drugstore. Everyone deserved to have qualified representation under the law.

After Dad's funeral, I stepped up the curb on Wilson Street in my black cowboy boots and black dress. My sister and I both bought boots to wear in his honor, our "Poppy" boots. I was relieved that his body's suffering was over. Approaching the front door, I remembered the unattributed packages we received that he sent: the stethoscope, the propane heater during COVID, the giant binoculars we called "ginoculars." I carried the dark green and gold urn into my house. Later I would carry the urn back down the steps and take it to my sister's house; he wanted to be under the oak tree in her backyard.

When I retired in fall 2023, I brought home a box of folders with the CMEC annual reports, documents I was proud of, and HR information that I'd need for tax time. I also carried grocery bags full of photos that I'd had on my office wall. They were vacation shots that inspired me to work, day and night, to be able to afford travel. In shifts, I carried the bulky bags up the curb and the walkway, up the front porch stairs, and into the house. I put them next to my computer. I thought, *Maybe I will write about those memories one day.*

Part V: What We Understand

All my life, I wanted to belong. I showed appreciation for my good fortune by being obedient, hard-working, and providing for others. Yet I was also different from my family — physically, emotionally, and sometimes philosophically.

I was head down with work and parenting when, unexpectedly, my father bet on ancient medicine to combat his Parkinson's diagnosis. Preparing to pick him up in India, I asked myself: When do we fight and when do we forgive?

I realized I had something to gain, and little to lose, by attempting contact with my biological relatives. Communications started with a carefully written letter sent as an email attachment by the adoption counselor. I chose truth over mystery. I overcame resistance and fear and was relieved at what I found.

Facing my past has reshaped the present and future for me, and for many dear people in my orbit. It gave me new appreciation for fallibility and imperfection, along with hope that wisdom will come with age for me, too.

I am grateful for all of it.

Sleeping on Dad's shoulder, 1968.

Handle with Care

India, 2015

In 2015, I flew forty-two hours to Coimbatore, India, to retrieve my weakening father after a five-week, Hail Mary stay. He hoped the Arya Vaidya Chikitsalayam Research Institute might cure his Parkinson's with the ancient secrets of Ayurveda, which incorporates everything from nutrition to yoga to lunar cycles into physical and spiritual healing.

Dad and his driver met me in Coimbatore. The airport was small and dusty, but Dad had a smile on his face. His white, short-sleeved shirt flapped in the wind as he opened his arms for a hug. We quickly left the dense clump of buildings and set out into the countryside. Palm trees lined the dirt roads, dotted with flowering copperleaf and Chinese hat plants.

Approaching the clinic, the Western Ghats loomed, spiky and covered with shades of green. Forested slopes provided roots and herbs essential to Ayurveda. Dad signed up for five weeks of treatment. I tried to learn about it, but Ayurveda seemed mysterious: remedies for cramps, headaches, or illness included deference to lunar positioning, herbs, massage, or head-shaving. On the long flight over, I wondered what I could learn about my Dad from spending time with him in this setting.

We settled into his cottage, where flying insects bumped into the light fixtures, and translucent geckos clung to the walls. Dad wore a white undershirt, briefs, and socks. His once-wavy locks were a spray of lonely hairs strewn across his scalp. He sat on a mattress, dictating memos to his assistant ten hours behind in Dallas.

Dad was a proud attorney and workaholic. He was at home in the courtroom and stood formidably before the judge's bench at six foot, four inches. His uniform for a six-decade-long career: dark slacks, button-down shirt, size thirteen wingtips, and a suit jacket.

Left: With Dad in India. Right: With Sloan and Dad at Half-Price Books, 2019.

Everything happened in the cottage, including meals. Dad handed me a menu in Tamil. I laughed when he pointed to an item saying, "This is rice," then moved his finger down. "This one is also rice."

A man entered wearing flared pants, a polyester shirt, and a newsboy cap. "Hello, Mista Frank. What would you like to eat?"

Dad asked, "What do you recommend?"

The man rattled off suggestions, and Dad exclaimed, "Perfect!"

When the gentleman left, Dad chuckled. "I have no idea what anything is."

A woman in a sari and sandals brought coffee and silver tins of food. The intertwined scents of coffee and cinnamon apples wafted up from the tray.

Dad was my hero when I was young, carrying me on his shoulders, amazing me by kicking a ball over our two-story house. He cheered me on through school, gymnastics, and piano. At 78, he was shorter, thinner. His lower lip hung as if to spill a secret, or apology. His cottage was spacious, our halves separated by space but not walls. It had been years since we shared a room. An attendant brought daily medicines — a tray of mysterious green liquids. Dad drank up and shrugged hopefully. "They're herbal." I practiced yoga for years, respected Ayurveda, yet was surprised that Dad had traveled so far for this alternative treatment.

The clinic was an oasis, a refuge from his cases back home, unpaid bills from underdog clients, and his second family draining his resources dry.

Lying awake with jet lag, I flashed back decades. When Dad dropped the bomb that blew up our family, he sat in the stately armchair in our living room, just redecorated by my elegant mother. He wore his suit; I wore my drill team uniform.

He declared he was selling the house, leaving me and my ten-year-old sister, and divorcing Mom for his receptionist. That night, from the upstairs window, I watched my shattered mother on the porch, hands shaking, begging, "Please don't go," as Dad slammed the yellow Cadillac door and screeched out of the circular brick driveway.

After I left home, Dad and I spent years with a frayed connection. But I never stopped yearning for his approval.

Eventually, we repaired the fracture when I needed legal counsel to establish my company and when I brought his grandsons into the world. He wrote the bylaws for my company's officers, and he surprised my boys with atlases and binoculars.

Drinking fresh coconut water, we sat on the porch shaded with palms and banyan trees. I asked him for stories. Dad remembered visiting his grandparents in Arkansas as a boy. He and his sister explored the woods with his snake-fighting terrier named Dicky. I pictured a barefoot kid in overalls, covered in scratches — Huck Finn at heart. Hearing this story, watching his weary body, I pondered his mortality.

A holy man knocked on the door, then entered. He marked Dad's forehead with curry-red chalk, handed him a magenta flower, spoke a cascade of words — a blessing — and left. I snapped a photo of Dad gazing out the window, white t-shirt absorbing the sun and framing his face.

The clinic's releasing doctor reported that Dad's hand strength had improved. He'd lost twenty-five pounds. His mind was clearer. The doctor cautioned that after a person receives Ayurvedic treatment, moving them is like moving a clay vessel filled to the brim with oil — viscous, but barely contained. I shored myself for the long trip home and for the proximity to his vulnerability, past and present. I worked to swap my anger about his betrayal for support.

Dad and I had recliners for the flight home. We shared meals and movie reviews. I left him in Dallas with a driver before I continued to Austin. I melted into his still-strong hug. I told the driver, "This is my dad. He has had a long journey. Please handle with care."

McLain family portrait on Mockingbird Lane.

Hoping Wisdom Comes with Age

Writing *Crowded Tables and Bonus Tracks* brought up some frustrations for me, primarily some latent anger over my parents' divorce. They separated when I was eighteen and divorced when I was twenty-one. I saw the impact on my mom and sister, and navigated between my parents for years, trying to keep relative peace. Not until I started working with a therapist at age fifty-three did I recognize my need for approval might have been seeded long ago, either when my dad left, or even as a baby awaiting adoption. Dad married his receptionist and took on parenting her two daughters more than us. They had challenges, including his wife's health, especially during and after COVID. Mom moved on with her career and with a second marriage, but even then, I didn't see her fully move beyond the sadness she felt at the loss of her first marriage. As the older child, I felt responsible to be a buffer even if I wasn't asked to serve in that role. I wanted the wound my father left in our family to heal, but I didn't spend time before now allowing myself to be angry or sad.

In recent years, Mom said she understood that Dad didn't have much freedom before they married; that he had to take care of his mom and sister, relatives, and us from a young age. I appreciated that observation, but it wasn't the same as resolution or resignation. I don't know if Dad ever apologized for leaving us. But what I did observe at the end of Dad's life was a kind of healing. I don't know if my parents would say healing occurred in their relationship, but the way they communicated with and cared for each other was far preferable to them not speaking, or saying terrible things about each other, or refusing to be in the same room. To the contrary. I admired the grace I saw in my parents at the end of Dad's life. What could I learn from them?

They'd known each other since they were in high school. They were each other's first loves and were married for more than two decades. Divorce created a rift for many years. But once J.C. and I had kids, our focus shifted toward them. We made sure they knew their six grandparents in Dallas and Austin, some closer than others. Years passed, and Mom nursed her second husband through his Alzheimer's, his time in a care facility, and until he died. She cared for her mother, my Gigi, until nearly her 100th birthday before moving to Austin to be closer to us.

When I focused on my family and career, Mom and Dad periodically leaned on each other in their roles as lawyer and decorator. Their respective professions, plus their joy at being grandparents, were stepping stones bridging the stream that separated them from each other. As age and time smoothed the sharp edges between them, Dad never failed to assist Mom with legal or contract matters, and Mom decorated Dad's private law office a few times over the years.

In 2021, we took Dad to Thanksgiving dinner at my brother- and sister-in-law Chris and Jennifer's home. Dad loved joining our whole family, who the Schmeils have generously included several times. In photos, dozens of people formed a large circle holding hands, expressing what we appreciated most. For many years, Dad's presence dominated any room, but there he sat in the frame of his walker while others stood, making him a head shorter than the people around him. He had a humble smile on his face: I could see he appreciated the happy spirit of the group, even if he missed his other family. It was a circle of love and acceptance.

Once Dad needed to move to Austin so Sloan and I could oversee his care as his Parkinson's was advancing, Mom offered to help. She didn't think twice about helping him figure out which furniture would fit in his assisted living apartment in SoCo Village. Along with myself and my sister, she was worried about Dad's health and visited the care facility with us to be sure we asked the right questions. The day of the actual move was chaotic. Dad's wife and her younger daughter packed up my stepmother's belongings for her move to Alabama, where she would live with her older daughter. They loaded Dad into the car and started driving to Austin. Meanwhile, I waited to hear from his movers. They called to tell me they would be late because none of Dad's belongings had been packed, which frustrated and saddened me. The movers kindly spent a couple hours hurriedly packing up his things (including dirty laundry) then headed for Austin.

Dad's wife and stepdaughter called on their way, expecting the care facility apartment to be ready for him by the time they arrived to drop him off then head to the Fairmont. I reminded them that the bed and furniture were on the way but delayed since the movers had to do the packing. They said they could not handle caring for Dad overnight at the hotel, even if I paid for a second room, since he would wake up frequently. So, once they arrived in Austin, my sister picked Dad up from the fancy hotel and took him to her house for the night.

Clearly, this was an emotional event for everyone involved. Dad's wife and her daughter hung out at the hotel bar. Meanwhile, Mom and I helped unpack the moving truck and direct furniture placement in the apartment. We worked until 3 a.m. organizing his clothes, making his bed, placing a few key sculptures and decorative items, and hanging paintings made decades ago by his mother, my Granny Esther. We placed flowers in a vase and rugs on the floor to make it as lovely as possible, though we knew he was sad to have to move into an "old folks' home."

The next day was worthy of a sitcom. While Mom and I were back at the apartment tweaking the decorations, Sloan called to say she was bringing Dad over. At the same time, she caught wind of my stepmother's coordinates (very close to the apartment) and sent me a red alert text. The last thing we needed at that moment was for the former wife (decorating his new apartment) and current wife (hungover and heading to say goodbye) to collide in this tender moment of parting after more than thirty years together. I hurriedly directed Mom out the back entrance of the building. We managed to avert the crash. My sister and I left Dad and his wife in privacy. Then she left with her daughter and headed to Alabama.

Dad was grateful to Mom, my sister, and I for preparing the apartment. However, we quickly found out that the décor needed to take a backseat to mobility considerations. Dad used to be over six feet tall and was still quite large, but now thin. His walker took up a lot of room and got caught on the rugs and decorative end tables. Soon, Dad and his caregivers rearranged everything. His recliner was in the corner by the window, next to a beautiful lamp and table, where he could place his iPhone, a tangle of charging cords, his meds, and the TV remote. The couch we had placed perpendicularly in the room had to be moved to the opposite wall for ballast. The heavy celadon vase by the door sat on the floor and housed walking sticks, umbrellas, and an antique saber. I had dropped off its marble stand at the Salvation Army because I knew it would have broken a foot if jostled and the vase were to fall.

For a few months, Dad worked in that apartment, still plugging away at his lifelong law career at the age of eighty-five. Grandson Sam did a noble job as Dad's replacement paralegal. Together, they handled a few cases and accounts, with papers strewn all over the floor. Though his body was failing from Parkinson's,

Dad's mind was still sharp, and the document chaos made sense to him. He loved his work, played blackjack on the iPad, and was delighted by visits from anyone (mainly me, J.C., Sloan, Julian, and Sam). There were a few activities at SoCo Village, like chess on Thursdays, but mostly he stayed in his apartment. COVID restrictions were still slowly being lifted.

Beckett's last visit with his Poppy included going through old black-and-white photos sent by his sister Jane, the McLain family's unofficial craftsperson (along with my sister) and historian. Jane McLain Wagley was a tiny, tough-as-nails woman living outside Fort Worth, a polio survivor who outlived two out of her three children and two of her many grandchildren. (She passed in June 2025.) After sharing the photos and stories, Poppy insisted on playing cornhole in the courtyard with Beckett. Dad made one bean bag into the hole while I stood behind him, praying he didn't tumble backward into me.

On sunny days, my sister brought Dad to her house. She is a gifted gardener, and Dad loved to help while she raked leaves, weeded, and placed miscellaneous metal creatures in the yard. One day, Dad demanded she drive him to Jerry's Artarama, where he purchased various spray paints. They went home, and he turned the metal armadillo, peacock, and cowgirl bright orange and purple and green. He bought Sloan programmable lights to shine into her massive backyard oak tree. Sitting under the biggest oak by a large fire, cozied up under a Mexican blanket with a beverage in hand made for a perfect evening.

In 2022, I was eyeballs deep in integrating my company into the acquiring company. Mornings were best for me, so I made a game of picking up sweets and coffee from the different coffee shops in my neighborhood and taking them to Dad to taste test first thing, along with giving him a big hug to start our respective workdays.

Mom's best friends in Austin lived in Northwest Hills. They were friends with my parents from law school. We all lived in Dallas when I was young, and we would see them because their kids were adopted like I was. For years after my parents divorced, Peggy and Jerry didn't see Dad but stayed close with Mom, especially after she moved to Austin.

When Dad moved to town, the friends insisted he come see them at their house. They had a beautiful pool, cantilevered out into the woods behind the house. Peggy, an angel of a person who lost the use of her left arm to polio when she was a teenager, loved my mom immensely. Mom would swim with her friend

Frank is welcomed in Austin for Thanksgiving.

each week, weather permitting, to help get her body moving as she approached 90, using lots of floaties and noodles.

When Mom offered to drive Dad to Northwest Hills for dinner, Dad said, "Can you go to Walmart and buy me a swimming suit?" Mom told me about that plan, and I thought it was crazy. I worried that she, at five feet, two inches, would not be able to help Dad if he lost his balance or fell. I imagined her trying to work with her friend and her one functioning arm, while keeping an eye on Dad, who had not been swimming in years. The lawyer friend would be no help, as he sat on the side of the pool in a chair, since his half-amputated foot was still healing. I told my husband about the swimming plan, and he said, "I can see the headline now: Four octogenarians tragically found floating in a pool in northwest Austin . . ." I strongly advised Mom against complying with Dad's wishes.

The next day, she confessed. She had indeed picked up a swimsuit for Dad and they all got in the pool. She did say he got away from her at one point, and she was nervous, but then he found his balance, and no mishaps occurred. I'm sure they told stories and cracked jokes from the pool deck. The foursome had snacks and a beer or a glass of wine. I like to think they were remembering old times with one another. It probably didn't feel like so long ago they were hiding Easter eggs for the annual hunt or taking us kids sailing. I wondered, and hoped, that Mom got some of the peace she needed from Dad after driving him home that night.

A month or so later, Dad got pneumonia and went into hospice at South Austin Hospital. I got the call during Corbin's Stanford graduation ceremony. At the time, I didn't know Dad was secretly crafting a shoe box lid into a diorama: Corbin in a tiny car racing toward his future on a road made of stapled one-hundred-dollar bills. It was Corbin's graduation gift.

The day Dad was admitted, he declared to the doctors, "I want to terminate this operation." He was done with his weak body and refused intervention, which we understood. That week, Sloan and Julian filled the room with flowers, music, a small magnolia tree, and his painted, metal garden sculptures. We played his favorite songs. Sloan and I compared our responses to grief. She felt her emotions deeply and visibly with buckets of tears, while I took care of business and maintained the stoicism that has characterized my personality during a crisis. The self-protection part of me was in full gear. Perhaps my biology was kicking in as well.

When Dad woke up a bit, midweek, he managed a flourish of updates to various legal documents, then asked for ice cream and Mom's homemade chocolate sauce, which she quickly prepared and brought to the hospital. Soon after, he sat up in a hospital chair in that stupid gown with a grin on his face, as we all — me, my husband, my sister and brother-in-law, and Mom — ate Bluebell vanilla ice cream with warm chocolate sauce out of paper cups. We all knew to sear that image into our memories, as it would be one of our last.

When Dad passed away a few days later, on the eve of Father's Day 2022, we toasted him with a whiskey drink my husband created called The Gambler, after Kenny Rogers' survival tale, which we later sang at his funeral. My wise friend Jenn said Dad "gets to be an ancestor now." I pictured him like a Macy's Thanksgiving Day Parade float, dressed like Big Tex from the Texas State Fair, hovering above and keeping an eye on all of us.

I hope I can keep love and forgiveness in my heart as I get older, especially if my life takes an unexpected turn. I'm now in this liminal space, after raising children, after my career, before whatever comes next. I realize there are not many of our parents' generation left, and before long we will be the elders of our families. What lessons and experiences will we pass along? What joys and struggles will our children recall? Where will we all be geographically when our bodies and minds start becoming frail, and will our kids worry over us?

I'm sorry to have missed that pool party, but I'm sure glad my parents ignored my advice.

Adoption Is a Box of Chocolates

At the memorial service for my Aunt Peggy, my lifelong friend (extended family, really) said something simple and striking. In honoring his adoptive mother, he started by saying that adoption is like a box of chocolates — you never know what you're going to get (courtesy of Forrest Gump). That statement captures a simple but stark truth about adoption. It's really a gamble for everyone.

In 1968, my parents and several of their friends all adopted kids for various reasons. The fathers were lawyers and handled the legal aspects of the adoptions for each other. We were a small pod of families prominent in my early childhood, and we all grew up knowing we were adopted. We were told that we were gifts, and this was a happy story. I came into my adopted family with a little handout. It was rather short and seemed like a CliffsNotes version of operating instructions for a baby: when to feed formula, when to bathe, that the little baby girl is "normal," etc. It included basic information about my biological parents, like hair color, a couple of their interests, and that they were twenty-one and twenty-two, both college students when I was born. It also said, "Likes to bathe, thinks it's fun," as well as, "Sleeps in a room with parents" (that phrase remains a mystery).

For me, being adopted was a basic fact, like having blonde hair. I never looked for my biological parents because I was content with my life, and I always felt grateful for the family who raised me. I never felt there were holes in my heart to fill. I was a dutiful child, and I still don't know if that's nature, nurture, or both. My parents had high expectations of me, but I was cared for and supported. Maybe I was a typical first-born child, or on a deeper psychological level, I knew that I could have ended up in a home with people less loving and generous than my parents. Perhaps even at a young age, I felt the need repay them for the life they'd given me.

I've heard a range of stories about adoption, including dramas on-screen. People told me their stories if adoption came up in conversation (my sister Sloan and I look very different). One friend reunited with a birth mother who had exhausted her support network and needed money, resulting in the end of

YOUR NEW BABY

Birthdate: 1-10-68 3:48 p.m. Birth Length: 18 inches

Birth Weight: 5 Lbs. 11 Ozs. Blood Type: O+

FEEDING: Formula: 13 ounces of Similac

13 ounces of water

Last feeding was at: 9 a.m.

Baby usually takes 3 1/2-4 ounces of formula every 4 hours.

6-10-2-6 p.m.—including night feedings.
Very little spitting.
Water: 2 oz. at a time between feedings.
Vitamins: 10 drops Poly-Vi-Sol directly in her mouth; she likes them.
She burps once a bottle.
She is a slow eater and likes a heated bottle.

SLEEPING: She prefers to sleep on her stomach, she sleeps in a room with parents; likes a night light. She sleeps most of the day, sometimes stays awake before a feeding and will stay in bed and look around, but she likes to be picked up and held, too.

BATHING: Johnson's baby soap has been used with success for baby's tub baths. She likes to bathe, thinks it is fun. She usually bathes before 9 or 10 a.m. feeding.

HEALTH: This baby is seen as a normal, healthy female infant.
Bowels: Normal, one movement in 24 hours.
General Health: excellent.

REMARKS: She likes a pacifier. Your baby is a cute little girl with a sweet disposition.

Care instructions from Hope Cottage.

communications. Another friend thought of their birth mother on their birthday every year, which I started to do after that conversation. That friend met her birth mother, with her adoptive mother attending the reunion. When the two mothers embraced, my friend said she felt deeply grateful to witness that mutual gratitude. Plus, she resembled her biological father, and he finally acknowledged paternity. Her story was moving but did not feel relevant to me at the time. I've heard stories about family disruptions and disappointments that arose from genetic testing exploration. I've heard that adopted people are disproportionately likely to become leaders or addicts.

My friend Joellen, an adult child of adoption and a psychologist, always encouraged me to look for my birth family — she said "genetic mirroring" (where the parts of you that come from your genetics are validated and supported) is important. She also explained that being a "gift" doesn't account for the birth mother's story as part of the adoption triad: adoptive mother, adopted child, and birth mother. It oversimplifies any complexities of her story by making it seem simple to gift a child to another person.

Joellen spent twenty years searching for and understanding her biology and family history, with complex and mixed results. She has committed her career to counseling those affected by adoption and volunteered her efforts to helping Texas-born, adopted adults gain access to their original birth certificates. Her adoption was a defining feature of her life and career, and she found medical knowledge, connection, and satisfaction from her search. She also knows many stories of trauma, so I was hesitant to dive into that world too deeply. She nudged but never pressured me.

When my parents were divorcing, and I was angry with my dad, I didn't think about being an adopted child. I was just a teenager with the rug yanked out from under me, so I wanted to escape from my home and the city where I'd lived my whole life.

Fast forward to 2021. Around the time my father's Parkinson's worsened, I was trying to keep my company afloat during COVID, dealing with friction in my work world, and confidentially working to sell the company. I also started regularly seeing a therapist. Early in our discussions, she made an observation around some of my tension with my male business partner — my agitation when we had a difficult work conversation, when I did not feel acceptance or approval, and when I cared too much about his opinion of me. She said, "No wonder. You were abandoned twice."

What?? I thought. She reiterated that I had been abandoned by my biological father and by my adoptive father through divorce. That revelation hit hard. For the first time, I was aware of the connection between those experiences, so distant in my past, and my anxious, teeth-grinding feelings during one of the most trying periods of my life.

A handful of times in the past, I joked cruelly that my bio mother could be a drug addict under a bridge. I postulated that she was not fit or able to be a parent, lacking money, employment, family support, or that she just didn't want me. Mostly though, I wasn't in touch with how I felt about being adopted and spending all of my life with people who weren't my birth parents. I simply hadn't let myself have many feelings on the subject. The exploration with my therapist turned out to be timely.

We discussed this more around the time I ran into a grad school friend at an Adoption Knowledge Affiliates event at our neighborhood brewery, ABGB. After the speaker finished, my husband and I milled around making small talk. I listened to a guy who found his birth parents because he didn't want to be an old person in a rocking chair wondering about them when it was too late. I pondered this while sipping my beer. Mortality was on everyone's mind due to the pandemic. My own father's decline was accelerating, and mom was healthy but in her 80s. Was it already too late to search for my birth mother? Was I afraid or curious? Would I hurt my parents by searching?

At ABGB during the Adoption Knowledge Affiliates event in spring 2021, J.C. was speaking with our friend from grad school. They started talking animatedly then hurried over to me with wide eyes. J.C. told me Marla was born on January 24, 1968, at Hope Cottage, an adoption agency based in Dallas in operation for about 100 years. When I told her I was there for three weeks — from January 10th to the end of the month of the same year — she exclaimed, "We were crib sisters!" We hugged each other tightly.

Shocked, I absorbed the revelation slowly. It was hard to fathom that we were at Hope Cottage at the same time more than fifty years ago. Literally, for the first time, I thought to myself: What was Hope Cottage like? Surely, we didn't share a crib, but were we in the same room? Or on the same floor? Unless we were with foster parents for those three weeks like newborn puppies, then we probably shared some newborn caregivers. My brain flooded with logistical questions, and it dawned on me that I probably spent more time with this friend than I did with my biological mother in the first days of my life.

Marla had reconnected with her birth mother and became close with a half-sister. I asked how she found them, explaining that I assumed a search required countless nights drinking Red Bull, combing the internet, scrolling through microfiche in some dusty library basement, or petitioning the court. Come to think of it, that's all that came to mind when I thought about looking for my birth mother — the arduous process, not the fact that she could be a real person with a unique story.

Marla explained that I could pay the agency, and they would look for my "Extended Information." After that, if I wanted the agency to handle the search and attempt contact, they could do so for a fee. I told her I was worried about taking time and energy away from my family. Aware that I was practically a workaholic, I feared feeling responsible for a birth family on top of the one I'd grown up with and the one I was raising. She understood my concern (as few people could), but she told me she believed there was no limit to the love you could put forth in the world.

After that night, I turned it over in my mind, feeling the weight of the choice in my hands. This new option was right in front of me — not an exhausting search, just some money. I thought: *I can afford that, but what other price should be considered? How would my mom, dad, and sister feel? My children, my husband?* I would ask for their blessing.

I shared the story of meeting my crib sister with the Goddess Collective. They enthusiastically agreed to join me in reading Ann Fessler's *The Girls Who Went Away* about birth mothers prior to the passage of Roe v. Wade, a book Marla called a "myth buster." The book featured dozens of first-hand stories from birth mothers who were sent away from their families to homes for unwed mothers, where they secretly completed their pregnancies and relinquished their babies. I talked through the stories and feelings with my book club, which importantly includes my sister.

Because *The Girls Who Went Away* was told from the perspectives of birth mothers, I was exposed to a wide range of individual stories that elicited a range of feelings in me: sadness, frustration, curiosity. The stories covered not only the birthing experiences of these mothers, but also their current situations. Some were happy and healthy with families; others never recovered from or forgave themselves for the imposed shame of giving up a baby. In the past, I'd said, "It's just biology," then thought anew, "It's biology!" I employed many wildlife biologists at the time in my company, so I knew its importance, and the connection clicked. A simple internet search revealed that biology means traits passed down for specialization and growth, development, metabolism, evolution, heredity, survival. It's adapting to environments of abundance and scarcity, resources, and stressors over generations.

Family portrait with my parents at 2 years old.

I began to realize the dominant narrative of the 1960s was that birth mothers were unfit to rear a child — too young, loose morals, irresponsible, strung out. Of course, able, A-list parents like mine could swoop in and give a child what they needed — a win-win solution. I discovered that based on my birth year, I was part of the "baby scoop era" between World War II and 1970, when two million babies were adopted in the US in the 1960s alone. Fortunately, my parents didn't speculate about my birth mother around me. They told me I was a precious gift, which simply made me feel special and prized.

Only when I read *The Girls Who Went Away* did I start to imagine my birth mother as an actual embodied person with a story. After finishing that book, I realized there was only one woman in the world who could tell me how I arrived on this planet. I decided I was ready to hear her story if she wanted to tell it.

The Letters

In June 2021, I reached out to Hope Cottage to request extended information about my adoption, based on advice from my "crib sister." What I received didn't include much new information, only that my bio father was Catholic. I wanted to know more, so I paid the fee and scheduled the required counseling session to have the agency attempt to contact my birth mother.

I had the counseling session via FaceTime on my cell phone while at a beautiful beach café in Greece. I had nothing to complain about and explained that to the counselor. They asked how I might feel meeting someone who looked like me. I'd always been curious. They asked how I might feel to learn sad or bad news, like if my birth mother or parents couldn't be found — a possibility if the information on file was out of date (due to address or phone number changes). The adoption agency had relocated in 1978, so files could have been lost or misplaced. After all, it had been fifty-three years since I was born. By the end of the call, I asked the staff to proceed with a search. And then I waited.

I got a call back while working in our Houston office. Imagine my surprise when the counselor at Hope Cottage quickly found my birth parents. That's right — parents. She called me and told me my birth parents wanted to make contact, and they were together. I hadn't even considered the possibility. When I told Joellen, she gave me a friendly punch in the arm and declared I had siblings. How could she know? She just did.

As recommended by the agency counselor, I wrote a letter to my bio mother and father that only included basic, non-identifying information. For a whole weekend, I wrote and deleted over and over, determined to find the right words and to keep them to one page. When I finally stopped fussing and let it go through the counselor out into the ether, my message conveyed that I had a career, a husband, two children, relatives nearby, hobbies, and a happy childhood. I did not include names, photos, or geography. I've been thinking about that term, "non-identifying." Generic. Average? That's in case one party or the other decides not to pursue further communication. What would lead to that? Would I receive a letter that confirmed my worst fears: That she was unfit to be a mother or wanted nothing to do with me? Surely, my counselor would prepare me for difficult news if that were the case.

But knowing that my biological parents were together, my fears lessened. In my non-identifying letter, I wrote:

> I have known my whole life that I am a gift. That has been a very simple fact, like the fact that I have blonde hair . . .

I went on to describe my family (generically), our occupations, and some hobbies. Then I wrote:

> Over the years, I have said that I want to write a thank you note to my birth parents for giving me the amazing life I've had through adoption, a life full of opportunities and loving people. I have assumed that there was not an ability to raise me, but there was never a dramatic story in my mind. I have never felt resentful or sad about being adopted – to the contrary, I have always felt very, very grateful.

I explained I had met someone from Hope Cottage and felt motivated to search for them. I added:

> I have always known that my birth mother kept me for three weeks. I know I was small, and I have dared to assume that I was being filled with love, hope, and dreams during that time. It must have been difficult to choose adoption, but I sincerely hope you were able to move forward with your young lives and pursue your aspirations.

I received a letter back from my birth mother in the middle of a road trip to drop our son off at Elon University in North Carolina. We drove as part of a two-car caravan with our close friends Jann, Randy, and Charlie. We were roughly halfway through the two-and-a-half-day drive when I checked my email on my cell phone and turned down the car radio. I looked wide-eyed at J.C., then turned around to Beckett, who was wearing his earphones in the backseat under a blanket. I said excitedly, "I just got an email from Hope Cottage with a letter attached from my birth mother! Want to hear it?"

Beckett replied, "Well, I'm listening to a podcast about Steve Jobs."

Really?! Teenagers.

I read the letter to J.C. My bio mother had asked the counselor for my name, and I had agreed. So, the letter stated:

> Dear Ashley, how wonderful to have a name! We were so happy to receive your letter. It filled us with joy, because it was all we hoped it would be… yes, we are happy and have had a wonderful life.
>
> January 10, 1968 — I've never stopped thinking about that tiny baby I held so long ago. Every year on her birthday, I would send out prayers into the universe, wishing her happiness and a good life. I confess I've always had a secret fantasy that someday I'd get a phone call… It was never a case of not wanting the baby; it was just what we felt we had to do… We were very immature, totally unfocused, and weren't ready… I knew we had to choose what was best for the baby and then get to work on ourselves afterwards… We finally became the couple I always hoped we could be.
>
> Your parents sound like wonderful people… I always thought I would like to thank them for accepting the most precious gift we could give them, and they have repaid us by giving you the life we imagined for you. Signing those papers was the hardest thing I've ever done. I held you twice in the hospital, and then someone cared for you until it was official. Had I been with you for three weeks, it would have been even harder. I remember trying to memorize your face as I told you I would love you forever, but you deserved a better life than we could offer… I always remind myself that we were not the people then that we are now.

They signed their letter "Karen & Jim."

From that first letter, I learned that, after a rocky start, they had created an enviable marriage and a strong family. They had two children, my 100 percent biological siblings, four years and ten years younger than me. Karen and Jim described their four grandchildren and their love for traveling and kayaking. I tried to imagine where one could kayak and go bass fishing. Their son went to the University of Michigan, which was one clue.

When we got to the hotel that evening, I asked Jann and Randy if they'd like to come to our room for a happy hour and told them I had something I'd like to share. J.C. poured us some wine in flimsy plastic cups, and we sat on the two queen beds. I read my letter first, then Karen's. While I read with a straight face and the stoicism that is my default mode when something stressful or emotional comes up, I looked up to see tears on Jann's cheeks. J.C. was leaning back against the headboard, taking it all in with a quizzical look on his face. I knew he would be supportive but was also concerned about our family's reactions to this huge news. It was also an out-of-body experience to suddenly learn the biography of my birth family. I watched my friends' reactions to the story to help me figure out how I should react. Most immediately, I didn't react with much emotion, but I had a lot of questions. And I had a lot more to share — if sharing good news was a relief to my bio parents, that was easy.

We had another day of driving to Elon University, and I knew we had to focus on Beckett — our youngest was leaving the nest. I was making lists of what he needed to set up his dorm room: clothes hangers, laundry baskets and detergent, toothbrushes and toothpaste, shampoo, deodorant, cold medicine, vitamins, and a basketball. At the same time, I was making mental lists of what I wanted to share and what I wanted to ask my bio parents. My mind was racing.

During the drive, I decided that everything about their letter made me comfortable sharing more information about myself. I was eager to see photos of my bio parents. Even though I was tired when we arrived at the second hotel, I stayed up late and wrote another letter, including photos of my family of four, my sister, mother, and father. I shared first names, but not last names. I didn't tell them we were in Austin, but they found out we were in Texas — I was born there, and they figured my lawyer father probably didn't move around for work. I sent that letter from my computer to the adoption agency liaison to put the exchange back in their court.

Once we arrived at Elon's beautiful campus, we concentrated intently on getting Beckett and Charlie settled into their college dorm room. I was sad to let Beckett go, but so happy that he was rooming with a lifelong friend; that the campus was full of trees and blooming flowers and ponds with students relaxing in hammocks; that we were emerging from the pandemic, and he'd have a little freedom.

Three years earlier when we dropped Corbin off at Stanford, J.C. teared up, while I was all smiles and proud for him to launch: I wanted to prove to Corbin that I could let him go because I knew he could thrive. With Beckett, I felt he was in the

Beckett skateboarding away.

right place. I wanted him to know that I trusted him to start building his own life. J.C., who is such a great and loving father, shed another tear. The last image in my mind (and the last photo I took of the trip) was Beckett skateboarding off through the tree-lined quad. With that, we were officially empty nesters.

When I got home, I wrote another one-page letter. This one to my mother and father, the parents who adopted and raised me. I had already told them I was interested in looking for my birth parents and had started the process. But I waited until I'd had time to digest the initial letter exchange before bringing them up to speed. I chose to write a letter because I didn't want to put Mom and Dad on a conference call to discuss this, and I didn't want to be there when they took in the news. I wanted to send them my reasoning and then go away while they absorbed what I shared. Fortunately, my sister was an excellent navigator for both of them as they absorbed my news.

Then I received two more long letters from Karen that included the backstory about their relationship: how she moved to Dallas to live with her sister until I was born and kept it a secret from most everyone else; how Karen and Jim worked on their relationship after she moved back to finish school in Ohio; how Jim proposed on the phone, they married two days after her graduation on a weekday, and Jim got orders to deploy to Vietnam a few weeks later. Clearly, I was born to a strong woman in addition to being raised by one.

Bio parents Jim Warden and Karen Martin dating, 1967.

Karen shared ample information about both their parents and grandparents (one a Norwegian, former interim North Dakota governor), and more about their upbringing and siblings. She shared some great photos and reported on the meeting with their two children, when they broke the news that they had a full-blooded sibling.

I could not have anticipated what happened next. In a matter of days, I received long letters with photos from both Wendy and Mike, my biological sister and brother. They were incredibly gracious and funny. Like their mother, they both wrote well. Wendy described the difficulty in starting her letter, procrastinating by straightening pencils, piling up the Kleenex. Mike talked about leaving the family dinner and dish-washing routine to sit down at his computer and wrap his mind around having another sister. He shared his daughters' reactions to learning this secret about their grandmother; one cried with sadness imagining how lonely their Nana must have been going through a pregnancy away from home and in secret. Wendy said her son Jack was excited to go from having a sister and two girl cousins to gaining two boy cousins to balance things out.

Mike's letter included this:

> Part of me wants to share our sense of humor by immediately sending you the calculus questions I needed some help on in high school... I also think about telling you how lucky we feel to receive this news and what a blessing it is that your life has been such a wonderful story. This whole thing was a shock, something we never suspected, never knew, and couldn't have dreamed of. We are so proud of our parents. They have been so vulnerable in sharing this story of a chapter we never knew. We have a new appreciation of just how strong my mom was at the time... She was with her sister Sonya, someone we always looked up to as a spitfire, fierce, independent woman. We now know she was also playing a caretaker role for my mom that has been a secret for 53 years.
>
> I think what makes me most curious is — knowing how much alike Wendy and I are, while being totally different — we wonder if you are alike in ways that we are, genetically. Your letters give us a big indication that you may be a whole lot like us. Thoughtful, dedicated, creative, loving, passionate, adventurous. Things we strive to be. If you want to connect with us, we're in...

Wendy wrote after reading the initial letter exchange between me and Karen:

> So many tears, cries of joy at the many crossovers in our lives and simply being stunned. No anger, no fear, just pure joy, wonder, and a huge amount of love for the bravery our parents had. We were floored that they were able to keep this a secret, but it wasn't their story to tell and once you reached out — they were so excited they could finally share.
>
> Looking through photos to share... Mom and I in Chicago, a photo fishing with my dad... And I have to remind myself that these are not things that you missed, they are a part of our wonderful life, and you have your own wonderful and amazing life that you have given us a glimpse into. I know it fills my parents with so much joy that everything they had wished for you, is true.

Their personalities shined through in their words, and I loved seeing their smiling faces in photographs. They both wrote with great pride about their work, their spouses, and their children. They both talked about the importance of music in their lives and proposed we share playlists. When Mike listed his favorite songs, I laughed out loud because we shared many of the same favorites (including Indigo Girls, The Avett Brothers, and Brandi Carlile). When I shared those with my husband, sister, and brother-in-law, we all made and shared our own playlists and got to know each other in a moving and joyful way. Being close in age, Mike and Sloan bonded the most over their playlists. I started referring to them — the playlists and the bio siblings — as "Bonus Tracks."

When Mike and Wendy realized they had a full sibling in the world, they almost hopped in the car to drive more than 1,000 miles from Michigan to Texas. Discovering siblings at 53, along with a younger generation of kids who quickly realize they're cousins, is a beautiful and humbling experience.

After absorbing the letter exchange, my mother wrote her own letter to my bio mother. Unsurprisingly, it was effusive, gracious, and kind. She shared photos of my first few years. She bragged about my academics and activities (lots of nurture). Among the many sweet paragraphs, these stand out as truly reflective of what kind of person she is:

> What an overwhelming revelation you have shared with us — there are so many ways our families are similar. I have faith in the hand of God touching lives; as I read about your family, I felt so grateful that we could share this story! We both have such wonderful families who enjoy being together and share many common interests! The only thing I do any differently is sail, which is a passion of mine; otherwise all enjoy travel, music, opera, art, and physical exercise!
>
> ... As I read your beautiful letters, I kept saying "Oh my gosh!" There were so many similarities!! Please know the gift of Ashley is, and was, the greatest gift ever given to me. When I add to that the gift of Susan [Sloan's first name — Sloan is a middle name], I am so grateful for my life with these two wonderful women who live their lives with such energy, courage, compassion, and love for others and the world around them!
>
> I hope we meet one day in the near future. It would be my great joy and blessing!!!

From all the letters, I was delighted to see many commonalities: The name James! It took me a while to register that Jim equals James. And my bio brother, James Michael, goes by J. Michael, just as my first son James Corbin (after grandfathers and relatives on both sides) goes by J. Corbin. Thomas Beckett (after Grandad Tom) also has a bio grandparent through Karen and Jim with a common name, Thomas. Jim's father was named Frank, like my father. Jim's sister was Sue, my mom's name. Karen and Sue (Jim's sister) were friends at Ohio State, and Sue introduced Karen to Jim. My mom lived in Toledo twice when growing up, and her parents attended Bowling Green State and Ohio State. Mom was planning to attend Ohio State before Dad convinced her to join him at the University of Texas. Jim and Karen dated on and off for four and half years before they married. Same with me and J.C.

Karen's sister Sonya cared for her when Karen, seven years younger, became pregnant. It was Sonya who initially contacted Hope Cottage for Karen. I am eight years older than my sister Sloan, and I did my best to support her when she became a mother.

Mike and I both studied overseas in Florence, Italy. Wendy's daughter dances like I did in high school (but much better). Wendy and I both played the flute (just two years in middle school for me). I took classical piano but stopped in college, while Mike was in the marching band at Michigan. Wendy and Jim both worked in education like my sister; my mom and aunt taught high school English.

In a letter, when Mike referred to his wife Mindy, he casually wrote that "the oak and the cypress grow not in each other's shade" to explain how they thrive as a couple. I sent him a photo of the wood and metal sculpture I had built for J.C. for an anniversary gift with Kahlil Gibran's *On Marriage* etched into the metal on the side — the source for the oak and cypress quote. That's how we found out that Karen and Jim chose the same reading for their wedding in 1969, as did Mike and Mindy, Wendy and Scott, and me and J.C.

One photo of Jim and Karen clearly in love is quintessential 1960s. He's sporting a turtleneck and mustache, and she's wearing a turtleneck and plaid blazer, with her straight blonde hair, plus a fringe of bangs.

When I dug around in my photo albums for photos to share with Karen, I found pictures of me and Mom with her rounded bouffant hairdo and a knit top. It struck me that, at the same time Jim and Karen got married, I was a one-year-old, and my mom was dressing me in frilly clothes and taping bows to my wispy-haired head. There was another baby picture that appeared to have been taken in a portrait studio at JCPenney or Olan Mills. Mom was formally presenting me to the camera, and I was wearing a lace gown that had been passed down in my family. When I looked at these photos of my first years with Mom and Dad, compared to the photos from Karen and Jim, I see the almost decade difference in age.

It dawned on me that I was a 60s baby, born in 1968, to bio parents who had been twenty-one- and twenty-two-year-old Ohio college students. In contrast, my adoptive parents were in their twenties in the late 1950s/early 1960s. When they adopted me, my mother was twenty-eight, and my father was thirty. He had started a legal career, and she was teaching and volunteering. They were settled in their lives in Dallas in the Bible Belt. My early life resembled a 1950s ethos in contrast to my biological parents' world of the 1960s and 1970s.

What would it have been like for me to become pregnant and consider having a baby at twenty-one? At that age, I was finishing college, unsure of my future occupation. I'd only had one semi-serious boyfriend and hadn't started dating J.C. yet. In the years between twenty-one and twenty-eight, I lived and worked in New York and San Francisco, moved to Austin, went to graduate school at UT, and got married. It would not be until I was thirty-two and thirty-five that I would be mature enough to have my own two children, and to balance motherhood with my marriage and career. I was eleven years older when I had Corbin than Karen was when she had me.

These thoughts flood my head whenever I reread these letters, especially the grace they gave me by saying they were ready for any level of communication I wanted to offer, with no pressure or obligation. My new bio siblings made a small but critical point of honoring my sovereignty and independence. Ironically, that statement of freedom has engaged me, rather than scaring me off after learning of the existence of an entire biological family up north in Ohio and Michigan.

Bonus Tracks

Mike and Wendy came for a visit to Austin just before Thanksgiving in 2021. We quickly connected and laughed over beers and barbecue. The next January, Karen came to Austin. We had a long lunch — we talked and talked, sharing stories of our families and comparing notes. We had a nice dinner with J.C. then the next day, I arranged for Karen to meet Mom.

The encounter between my adoptive mother and bio mother astonished me. Their meeting for tea became a four-hour discussion at Mom's beautiful Austin apartment. My mothers (!) shared their gratitude for each other. Mom directly asked Karen if she thought about going back to get me since she and Jim ended up together just a year after I was born. Karen said no, they felt confident in their decision, with the hope that I would end up in a wonderful family. Karen was so glad to meet my mom Sue and has called her "my hero."

The one thing that was too much for Mom was over coffee the next day when Karen started showing us photos of relatives who resembled me. Though she said nothing, just that she had to be somewhere, I think Mom felt protective and feared my bio family thought resemblance implied staking a claim for me.

A month later, we planned a trip with my sister and Mom to go to Michigan to meet Jim and the bio siblings' families. I quickly learned that Jim is very easy going. In February 2022, when we first met in an Ann Arbor coffee shop near where Mike and Wendy live (they're all about an hour apart from one another), Mike sat me and Jim down at a quiet table for two in the back. After a couple awkward minutes, I asked Jim gently yet directly if he was relieved when Karen chose adoption back in 1967.

His response was, "You were meant to be born into love," whether I was going to end up with him and Karen, or their parents, or someone else. I found this to be perhaps the most beautiful thing he could say to me. At the end of the weekend, I connected Dad with my bio father on FaceTime. I watched and listened

Top: Meeting Jim and Karen, my bio parents. Bottom: Together with my siblings.

as Jim said to my dad, "I want to shake your hand," and said he and Karen planned to visit in the fall. They both said a hearty "thank you!"

I know my father was grateful to meet Jim, if only on FaceTime; sadly, Dad passed away before they could meet in person. When Karen and Jim came for their visit, we hosted a nice buffet dinner where they were able to meet more members of my Austin family, standing around our kitchen island, as if this kind of thing happened all the time.

Now a few years in, I know I don't want my bio parents to redirect or reallocate any love or attention away from their two kids and four grandchildren toward me or my children. I don't want them to imagine or romanticize stories about me or claim my attributes. If anything, I want my bio siblings to be closer to their parents and to each other as a result of learning about me.

Acknowledging that we all have some fears and insecurities, I want Karen and Jim to feel relieved that they can share the truth about a scary time in their young lives and fledgling relationship. It's especially important to me that my biological mother, who endured her secret pregnancy and gave birth in Dallas with just the support of her sister, feels free to share her truth after I connected with her and confirmed that her choice had been a good one.

After reconnecting with Karen, while traveling in Ireland in 2024, I heard the words to a song by The Smiths with new ears. "This Night Has Opened My Eyes" includes these lyrics:

> The dream has gone
> But the baby is real
> Oh, you did a good thing
> She could have been a poet
> Or she could have been a fool
> Oh, you did a bad thing
> And I'm not happy and I'm not sad
> A shoeless child on a swing
> Reminds you of your own again
> She took away your troubles
> Oh, but then again, she left pain
> Oh, please save your life
> Because you've only got one

I wrote my bio mom a postcard about it. I said she did a good thing — in my case, placing me up for adoption (regardless of any other interpretation of the song lyrics). When I heard the line about "a shoeless child on a swing reminds you of your own again," it struck me that my bio mother must have tracked my age at each birthday . . . for more than half a century. She very well could have had this experience of seeing a child on a swing and wondering where I was, how I was, what I was doing, what I looked like. In one letter, she said when visiting Sonya in Dallas, and even when managing her sister's things after she died, Karen wondered if she ever passed me on the street. I would have liked to meet Sonya to thank her, too.

I feel both peace and relief knowing that my biological mother is a happy, healthy person in a strong relationship with a loving family. Jim is clearly a devoted husband, father, and grandfather. I confess I am still fearful that I might hurt my Mom somehow, so I try to set boundaries for both of our families. We don't exchange gifts but send an occasional card. I send them wine on Thanksgiving.

Nature and nurture both affect how a child becomes a spouse and a parent. Through my writing, I recognized that I had a loving father until I was eighteen. I also had one after that, but I didn't want to support his choice of a different family over ours. I didn't want to accept my mother's disappointment at being left by my father. For years, I declared that I didn't want to be a wife because it seemed like a crappy job. I observed that even if you are healthy and well-dressed, active and generous in the community, keep a gorgeous house, and are a wonderful cook and mother, a husband can get lured away and walk out, leaving a delicious meal to languish in the warming drawer, abandoning you to figure out how to pay the bills, raise the kids, tell the hard truth to your friends, and start over.

Interestingly, it was when Mom stepped down from being a paragon of perfection that she became more human and approachable to me and my sister. She built an outstanding career as a decorator with a keen eye, faithful contractors, and admiring clients. She enjoyed a good relationship with her second husband, the Episcopal priest with grown children who thankfully are lovely people and relatable to me and my sister. Now in her mid-80s, she maintains exceptional personal style and rock-solid commitment to health and adventure.

Obviously, I overcame my resistance to becoming a wife; I accepted that agreeing to marry came with the risk of divorce, the toll of which I had witnessed firsthand. After four years and seven months of dating, plus a year of engagement, J.C. and I celebrated thirty years of marriage on June 24, 2025. Because he came from very stable parents, and because I came from divorce, we brought a combination of trust alongside the awareness that you can't take a relationship for granted. You must work on it; you have to appreciate each other. My bio parents, after placing me up for adoption, proceeded to marry the next year and have now been married fifty-five plus years. As their letters clearly stated, they chose to work on their relationship prior to marrying or having (more) children. Perhaps I have a biological predisposition to commitment.

Jim said I was meant to be born into love. I believe I was. And though at times my parents' love for each other was imperfect or impermanent, they were amicable at the end of Dad's life, and they offered each other solace. Even when there was distance between me and Dad, my parents' love for me was steadfast.

I'm still figuring out how I want to interact with my biological family. I flow between eagerness and interest, and protection and self-preservation. At times I want to retreat to my place of comfort, surrounded by my "real" family who raised

Left: Jim Warden in Vietnam in 1969. Right: Beckett in Vietnam in 2025.

me, to protect them from worry or speculation about what my relationship will be with my bio family in the future. There's no question that my biggest fear is likely shared among us all, that we'll stretch ourselves too thin, compare ourselves in unhealthy ways, or place obligations on one another.

I used to think: What will it cost me to look? Now I know I would have paid a price if I had not looked. I would have missed out on an important part of the story. It's not just my story, it's our story — my bio parents, siblings, their kids, and my adoptive parents, cousins, my sister's family, her kids, my husband, and our children. Before Beckett left for a three-week trip to Vietnam in January 2025, we FaceTimed Jim and Karen. Beckett talked about his itinerary exploring the whole country, and Jim shared his experience serving in the Vietnam War. Just six weeks after they married on St. Patrick's Day in 1969, Jim was called up to Vietnam as part of the Army Reserves in a medical dental unit. He got out after a few months and went to graduate school. I have seen a photo of Jim in his Army fatigues: with his curly mustache and stately nose, Jim resembled my Beckett around the same age. I know my bio parents followed Beckett's trip through photos on Instagram. Beauty and hope come through the photos of the students immersed in this cultural exchange, predicated on forgiveness of the past and commitment to evolving forward.

I understand I was born to a young woman who knew she didn't want to marry a man who wasn't ready, and she didn't have the means to raise me alone.

Photo from my baby book with description of legal adoption celebration on October 8, 1968.

She was practical, in a sense, and not willing to abandon or sacrifice herself. She was fortunate to have a sister living outside Dallas and was able to live there in privacy until I was born. She took correspondence classes and told her parents she needed space from her boyfriend but did not reveal her pregnancy. She had some counseling from Hope Cottage and gave birth to me two weeks early, breech, at the Methodist hospital. She signed the adoption papers on January 24, 1968 (on my due date, two weeks after I was born, coincidentally J.C.'s birthday). She took a German Shepherd puppy home to Ohio and got on with her life. She finished her degree at Ohio State. Within the next year, she was engaged to and married Jim, who then was called to Vietnam. Thankfully, he came back.

Meanwhile, on February 1, 1968, I was handed over to my elated mother and father. Somewhere, there is a photo of a big matronly woman from the agency preparing to hand over a tiny, swaddled baby — me. There are pictures of my radiant mother and a meticulously prepared nursery, adorned with a silver baby hairbrush and rattle. She looks completely put together and not tired, in contrast to a biological mother's state of exhaustion after giving birth. On my official legal adoption day in October 1968, my arms are stretched out wide, inviting my parents to pick me up and hold me.

We have fading old photos in albums. Many informal photos show me with my dad, sleeping on his lap or shoulder, him holding me with a forearm, him tossing me in the air. Images of me and my cousins and later my sister show us climbing trees, watched by our doting grandmothers in their cat-eyed glasses and floral

Top: Me, Mom, and Sloan with the Wardin-Martin family. Middle: Christmas in Steamboat with the McLains, Schmeils, Waits, and Dockerys. Bottom: Christmas in Steamboat with the Schmeils.

dresses. The bulging albums spill over with pictures documenting my upbringing. There are team photos from soccer and gymnastics; photos of me in a foot or arm cast; me and my sister playing the piano; friends and family enjoying vacations at the Texas coast or in the mountains, swimming, skiing, or leaning off the bow of a sailboat reaching up to feed the seagulls. I have been loved.

We all have truths and mysteries in our lives. I turned over the record of my known world, and looked for, listened to, the other sides — the bonus tracks.

Appreciating small surprises along each new path.

Holiday lights on Alpenglow Way in Steamboat Springs.

Epilogue: Gratitude

On January 10, 2025, I celebrated my 57th birthday. It was a beautiful day. Mom got me nice workout clothes, I indulged in a wheel pottery class, had a massage, and opened too many presents from my husband. I enjoyed great food and live music with Sloan, Julian, and J.C. Our sons sent me flowers.

The next day, I got a card from my biological mom Karen. It said: "January 10th doesn't make me sad anymore — now it's just a happy day of celebration!" I know I'm lucky to get that card, symbolizing a unique sense of coming full circle: Finding the woman who had to let me go, connecting her to the woman who raised me, understanding that it took both people for me to live my story.

I also got an email from my bio father Jim. He said, "I remember the day you were born. Karen's sister called. We had a code name for you. It was Winston. She said, 'Winston has arrived.' Happy birthday." I love that simple, funny message and know that I was blessed with a caring biological father in addition to my dad.

Sitting and writing in Colorado, in our dream house we have filled with family and friends, gazing at the snowy peaks of Emerald Mountain and Sleeping Giant, I know fate and free will, nature and nurture have played their roles in getting me to this place in a life that I'm fortunate to share. With my feet on the Earth, surrounded by evergreen trees, watching the alpenglow sunset, I feel spiritually rooted, fascinated by the natural world, and still committed to environmental stewardship. I now understand I'm best served through a combination of wonder, gratitude, and acceptance for the opportunities I've received and the entities I've built: both what I've inherited and what I've created.

The advice to be irreverent motivates me to try new things like creative nonfiction writing. It helps me switch from "why?" to "why not?" thinking, from "why does my story matter" to "why doesn't my story matter?"

This story is my way of saying thank you.

Your story matters, too.

Acknowledgments

I am deeply grateful to my family and friends for supporting me in writing *Crowded Tables and Bonus Tracks*. Without the gentle suggestions from my friend Joellen over decades, I would not have attempted contact with my bio family. If we hadn't run into Marla at ABGB, I would not have considered searching and would have failed to meet the truly wonderful people who are my biological family.

I humbly thank my cofounders at CMEC, the wonderful staff who made us strong, and the leaders who took over the reins so I could step down — especially Emily, Meghan, Chris, Ryan, Haley, and Susan.

I took a variety of writing classes before starting this manuscript and learned a bit from each teacher. I am especially grateful for the patience and wisdom provided by my coach, Cecily Sailer. She helped me switch off my deadline-focused work brain, consult my heart and not just my head, and let the writing process itself guide me. My editors at d'Aulnoy Editions have been encouraging while providing expert guidance on structure, order, and what to leave out. I'm humbled that Publisher Michelle Newcome at White Deer Publishing was willing to take a chance and partner with me for this project.

Now I'd like to offer a shout out to some very influential groups of people.

Finding My Tribes

I heard a quotation one time that said, "If you want to save the world, save the women." I believe it to be true. Though I have wonderful relationships with the men in my family and many men in my life, the tribes of women around me deserve special recognition for making me who I am today. We show up for each other with whatever it takes — soup, bourbon, or deep breathing in community.

WTS International — Women's Transportation Seminar — Heart of Texas chapter was the first professional tribe I joined. WTS was founded in 1977 to advance women in the transportation field through professional development, encouragement, and recognition. The Heart of Texas chapter grew from a small group in the late 1990s to a formidable professional organization in the 2000s. When I was opening my own firm, I leaned into WTS. Over the years, I served on several committees and as Southwest Region liaison. Over my twenty-five plus years of consulting (including twenty plus years in WTS), the only single-company award CMEC received was a WTS Employer of the Year award.

In 2016, just before our company's tenth anniversary, I received the Woman of the Year award from WTS based on member votes. It's the most public and industry recognition I have ever received. I am genuinely grateful. I invested in WTS since the male-dominated business atmosphere still presents a steep incline for professional growth and compensation equity for women. In 2024, J.C. and I gave a gift to the WTS Scholarship Fund.

Through WTS, I was admitted to the Women Business Owner's Roundtable, a group of impressive women leaders who taught me about strategy and management. Colleagues from that group influenced how I helped lead CMEC through COVID and connected me to the agency we hired to sell our company.

The other tribe of women that has been essential for my successful company exit is HiPower, whose goal is to help women go from success to significance. Founded in 2012 in the California Bay Area, HiPower launched in Austin in 2019. I joined the Signature Program that year, along with a dozen women executives from a variety of fields who develop and pursue personal platforms.

The activities in the Signature Program enabled me to see my career from a higher altitude for the first time, prompting me to create my first elevator speech:

- Our firm is devoted to "environmental stewardship" . . . that is, finding the balance between modernizing infrastructure and protecting our precious environmental resources.
- We are specialists who collaborate with engineers and regulators to design infrastructure solutions that avoid and mitigate adverse impacts on our vulnerable world.
- Together we forge solutions for 2040, 2050, and beyond . . . with long-term impact in mind.
- I'm passionate about the work we do — I've done it for more than twenty years — because I firmly believe we are creating a better world for future generations.

This platform was heartfelt and became a key part of articulating our company culture when we came to the juncture of needing to sell. The encouragement from other women in HiPower — from different industries such as law, medicine, and tech — enlightened and motivated me. These women helped me harness my personal power, beyond being dutiful to my cofounders, beyond trying to impress my father, beyond ensuring my family was well-situated financially, and beyond my perceived limitations. Deciding to seek out my birth parents and writing my story are outgrowths of the motivation and inspiration I gained from HiPower. The founder interviewed me and covered our successful exit in the excellent *Sail to Scale* by Mona Sabet, Heather Jerrehian, and Maria Fernandez Guajardo. I am paying this experience forward as a HiPower executive to amplify other outstanding women in their journeys.

Two personal tribes have provided community and support for me for years. After coming back from living in Paris with J.C., a friend and I started a book club. A dozen women started meeting monthly to discuss a book and share a potluck. The group has morphed over the years, but we recently celebrated our twenty-eighth year together. We have shared relationship wins and losses, parenting journeys, and the challenges of being the sandwich generation. We've read close to 300 books together. In 2021 when I approached the book club to find out if they wanted to read *The Girls Who Went Away* by Ann Fessler, about pregnant women who were sent to homes to have their babies prior to the Roe v. Wade decision legalizing abortion, they enthusiastically agreed and were there to support me when I decided to search for my birth parents.

We call our book club the Goddess Collective. It's a tongue-in-cheek moniker but also aptly describes our mutual admiration society. The name originated as follows: One of J.C.'s architecture buddies had started a stint of meeting the guys at the Yellow Rose strip club. I had expressed my anger and frustration to him — why were these brainy architecture grad students doing this, and why now? That was early 2000, and I was pregnant with Corbin. I confided in my book club. As always, we had a lively debate about the subject and waxed philosophically. One member mentioned she had a friend who played music at a strip club, and why didn't she ask him to get us in to investigate? So, there we were, the book club, waiting on a Monday night at the entry door of now long-gone Crazy Lady Strip Club on the I-35 frontage road. As he ushered us inside, the musician friend referred to our group as the Goddess Collective, and the name stuck. Suffice it to say we had an eye-opening experience at the club that dispelled some of my fears and insecurities. What has lasted is the name Goddess Collective and a stellar group of women I've enjoyed meeting with over books and wine approaching three decades.

Finally, Yoga Mamas is very important to me. A dozen years ago, a mother friend in our beloved Travis Heights neighborhood attended a yoga retreat in California, then decided to bring a similar retreat to the Austin area. For years, we've met for a weekend in the winter (usually January) at the Margaret Austin Center, now the Houston Zen Center. It's a sleepaway camp for grown-ups: the main building has several connected and angled wings, constructed of wood, with bunk beds and a huge communal kitchen. With the exception of COVID times, a core group of neighborhood moms have met to practice yoga, share stories, cook food, make vision board collages, and open up to each other about what's happening in our lives. This annual weekend is a wonderful reset to prepare for the challenges of the year to come. This is a warm, loving, safe space for all of us, and I receive a huge infusion of community and connection from my Yoga Mamas.

These tribes of women have supported me, helped me grow, taught me how to be vulnerable and grateful, and enriched my life in ways that have become essential to my well-being. The song "Crowded Table" by The Highwomen plays in my head while I write this. It's a tribute to my tribes and the dream for our Colorado home.

> I want a house with a crowded table
> And a place by the fire for everyone
> Let us take on the world while we're young and able
> And bring us back together when the day is done

Resources

- Adoption Knowledge Affiliates
- Support Texas Adoptee Rights

The Goddess Collective, 1997 to present.

www.ingramcontent.com/pod-product-compliance
Ingram Content Group UK Ltd.
Pitfield, Milton Keynes, MK11 3LW, UK
UKHW062312290726
14090UKWH00018B/1030

9 781945 783487